LEADING
YOUR
CHURCH
THROUGH
CHANGE

LEADING
YOUR
CHURCH
THROUGH
CHANGE

*A guided workbook for pastors
and their leadership teams*

BRIAN HARPELL

Published in partnership with Action International Ministries
PO Box 398, Mountlake Terrace, WA 98043
actioninternational.org

TABLE OF CONTENTS

ACKNOWLEDGEMENTS

In September of 2011, I was asked to speak at a conference held in Moa, Cuba on the subject of leadership. It was an incredible and unforgettable experience.

The materials were received so well, that before the conference wound down, sponsors of the conference were asking about the possibility of producing the materials in a book format, so that other pastors and leaders could benefit.

This workbook is the result of that request, which came from Lester Acosta, Vice President of the Baptist Convention of of Eastern Cuba; his wife, Raquel; my interpreter David Gomero, founder of Traducciones NaKar; Brian Stewart, Director of Action International Ministries; and Eddy Gonzalez, Rector of the Baptist Seminary in Santiago de Cuba and Pastor of the Third Baptist Church in Santiago de Cuba.

I agreed to the project on one condition: that we would work together as a team in collaboration. I would write the materials, David would translate the materials into Spanish, Raquel would contextualize the materials for the Cuban culture, while Brian and Action International Ministries would oversee the design, printing and distribution of the book.

What you have in your hand is the collaborative work of many people and the first step in our international mission vision of Cuba for Christ. We pray that this workbook would be a blessing to you and your congregation.

I want to thank my wife, Lynne, my family, Eddy Gonzalez and my Cuban Leader Learning Community for their hard work of editing for this second edition of the book, and the First Baptist Church in Everett, Washington for supporting my numerous mission trips to the beautiful island of Cuba. Without your partnership, along with the many relationships I enjoy with my brothers and sisters in Cuba, this book would not have been possible. Thanks team!

—Brian Harpell

INTRODUCTION TO LEADING YOUR CHURCH THROUGH CHANGE

We live in a world saturated with change, a world where the only constant is change. Unfortunately, the church has a reputation for being one of the last places to embrace change. Some congregations, trying to avoid the reality of a changing world, decide to live in the past. Others attempt to grip tightly to the *status quo*. But whether we admit it or not, the *status quo* is a myth. To stand still in a world, where everything is changing and at an ever-increasing rate, is to be left behind.

What is needed in a change-saturated world, are men and women skilled in effectively leading transformational change. This workbook is about how to lead and navigate change toward God's vision. This book, relying upon best practices in both the church world and the business world, addresses the relevant issues related to leading change such as: How do you arrive at a vision for the future? How do you introduce the need for change? How do you go beyond the first steps of change? How do you build and sustain momentum? And how do you lead toward God's vision as a team?

Leading Your Church Through Change is a work book study of the Old Testament leader, Moses. Moses was an incredible leader of transformational change, leading the Israelites from bondage in Egypt on the long journey to the Promise Land. Moses' story is a model for leading transformational change.

While *Leading Your Church Through Change* is a study about leadership, it is also a Bible study designed for individual leaders and is most effective when studied with a group of leaders. Each chapter has three sections:

- An *EXPOSURE* section where the reader is exposed to Scripture and leadership principles.
- An *EXERCISE* section where the reader is invited to complete an exercise related to the material presented in the *Exposure* section.
- An *EXPERIENCE* section where the reader is encouraged to participate in a group experience. The *Experience* section takes the material to an important next level. Leadership is not a solo enterprise, and it is why I strongly urge readers to involve a small group in this adventure.

One of the emphases in this book is that leadership is best done as part of a team. We can all learn from one another. As you begin to implement some of the leadership principles of this book, I want to encourage you to share your own learning and experiences with me. You can contact me through brian@brianharpell.com

Partners in His Adventure,
Brian Harpell

CHAPTER 1

GOD BEGINS WITH A LEADER

Exodus 1

KEY PRINCIPLE: GOD ALWAYS BEGINS WITH A LEADER TO SERVE AS A CATALYST FOR CHANGE.

"Nothing is more important than the leadership."
—George Barna, *Leaders on Leadership*

EXPOSURE: The leadership of Pharaoh

As we begin this study on Leading Your Congregation Toward God's Vision, we will be looking closely at the life of Moses as his story comes to us in the book of Exodus.

The book of Exodus is one of the five books of the Pentateuch. The word *EXODUS* means *"departure"* or *"going out."* The book of Exodus is the story of God's leading the people of Israel out of bondage in Egypt toward the Promise Land, through His chosen leader, Moses. What we see in this story is that God always chooses people—God's choices are often surprising, as we will see—to lead in accomplishing His purposes.

The book of Exodus opens by reminding us of Joseph and his family (the twelve tribes of Israel) residing and multiplying in Egypt.

> **Exodus 1:1-8**
>
> *¹These are the names of the sons of Israel who went to Egypt with Jacob, each with his family: ² Reuben, Simeon, Levi and Judah; ³ Issachar, Zebulun and Benjamin; ⁴ Dan and Naphtali; Gad and Asher. ⁵ The descendants of Jacob numbered seventy in all; Joseph was already in Egypt. ⁶ Now Joseph and all his brothers and all that generation died, ⁷but the Israelites were fruitful and multiplied greatly and became exceedingly numerous, so that the land was filled with them. ⁸ Then a new king, who did not know about Joseph, came to power in Egypt.*

These introductory verses from Exodus 1:1-8 span a long period of time. According to most ancient historians, Joseph came to leadership in Egypt around the beginning of the 13th Dynasty and died around the end of the 14th. Many ancient historians believe Ahmose[1] to be the *"new king"* referred to in Exodus 1:8, *"who didn't know Joseph, [who] came to power in Egypt."* Why didn't he remember Joseph? Because hundreds of years had passed in these early verses of Exodus.

One of the great themes of the book of Exodus is the theme of leadership. This theme is introduced in chapter 1, verse 8, with THE LEADERSHIP of PHARAOH. Being the king of Egypt, Pharaoh was obviously in a position of leadership. So, let's look closer at the leadership of this Pharaoh.

> **Exodus 1:9-14**
>
> *⁹ "Look," he said to his people, "the Israelites have become much too numerous for us. ¹⁰ Come, we must deal shrewdly with them or they will become even more numerous and, if war breaks out, will join our enemies, fight against us and leave the country." ¹¹ So they put slave masters over them to oppress them with forced labor, and they built Pithom and Rameses as store cities*

---

[1]   During the three Egyptian Dynasties (15—17th), the region experienced a period of decline as the land was invaded and ruled by the Hyksos (Hick-sohss). However, in the beginning of the 18th Dynasty, the Pharaoh Ahmose expels the Hyksos (around 1550 BC), marking the start of the rejuvenated kingdom which would eventually be recognized as the heyday of Egyptian power and splendor.

for Pharaoh. ¹² But the more they were oppressed, the more they multiplied and spread; so, the Egyptians came to dread the Israelites ¹³ and worked them ruthlessly. ¹⁴ They made their lives bitter with hard labor in brick and mortar and with all kinds of work in the fields; in all their hard labor the Egyptians used them ruthlessly.

The Hebrew population living in Egypt was exploding and, as we all know, there is might in numbers. Clearly these numbers worried this new king; caused him fear and threatened him. In addition, Egypt had enemies who bordered them. It's one thing to defend your country from an outside attack, it's quite another to be vulnerable to attack from the inside.

This new king was obviously militarily minded and recognized a potential alliance between the Hebrews and any of their bordering enemies. Thus, in verse 11, we learn of his first attempt at preventing such an alliance: *"So they appointed taskmasters over them to afflict them with hard labor."* This Pharaoh was a hard taskmaster of a leader.

Leadership has to do with our influence or impact on others, which can be either positive or negative. In the case of Pharaoh's influence, his leadership was negative. Having this in mind, let's look at what is involved in positive leadership. This might be a good time to define what we mean by the term *"leadership."*

EXERCISE: Defining leadership

What is leadership? There are a variety of definitions of leadership. Read each of the definitions below and circle the word or phrase which resonates with you regarding the meaning of leadership.

> ► *"Leadership is doing the right thing."*
> Warren Bennis and Burt Nanus

▶ *"Leadership is figuring out what needs to be done and then doing it."*

Anderson, *Leadership that Works*

▶ *"Leadership is when persons with certain motives and purposes mobilize, in competition or conflict with others, institutional, political, psychological, and other resources so as to arouse, engage and satisfy the motives of followers."*

James McGregor Burns

▶ *"Leadership is getting others to want to do something that you are convinced should be done."*

Vance Packard

▶ *"A leader is a dealer in hope."*

Napoleon Bonaparte

▶ *"Leadership is a relationship—a relationship in which one person seeks to influence the thoughts, behaviors, beliefs or values of another person."*

Walter Wright, *Relational Leadership*

▶ *"A leader is a person with God-given capacity and God-given responsibility who influences a group of followers towards God's purposes for the group."*

J. Robert Clinton, *The Making of a Leader*

▶ *"Leadership is mobilizing others toward a goal shared by the leaders and followers."*

Garry Wills

▶ *"Leadership is influence."*

J. Oswald Sanders, *Spiritual Leadership*

Which one of these definitions resonates or connects with you? Do you have a favorite? Each definition provides a perspective on leadership, that can enhance our understanding of leadership.

Using the words and phrases you circled in the exercise above, write your own personal definition of leadership:

Leadership is _____

_____

_____

_____

_____

_____

_____

To avoid a lack of clarity and confusion, I want to provide the following definition of leadership that I will be operating from through this study:

> *"A leader is a person with the ability to influence a specific group of people in a specific direction."*

Now, there are all kinds of leaders. This Pharaoh in the book of Exodus was a person with the ability to influence a specific group of people in a very specific direction. He used his power and authority to bring hardship on the people of Israel. Pharaoh's leadership style can be summed up in one word: Pharaoh was the *"boss."*

Here is a key truth I do not want you to miss in this story: Hardships experienced by God's people never go unnoticed by God!

In Exodus 2:24-25 we read, *"God heard their groaning... So, God looked on the Israelites and was concerned about them."* Listen! Effective leaders are attentive to what their followers are saying. How well do you listen to the people you are leading? Are you listening?

EXPOSURE: *The leadership of Shiphrah and Puah*

"But the more these slave-drivers afflicted them, the more they multiplied and the more they spread out . . ." (vs. 12). Pharaoh's "Plan A" didn't seem to be working. So, Pharaoh devised a "Plan B" that was even more reprehensible! Pharaoh, to curtail the burgeoning Hebrew population, decreed that every male child born to a Hebrew mother should be drowned in the Nile River. He ordered Egyptian midwives, including— Puah and Shiphrah—to abort all the Hebrew male babies.

Exodus 1:15-22

[15] The king of Egypt said to the Hebrew midwives, whose names were Shiphrah and Puah, [16] "When you help the Hebrew women in childbirth and observe them on the delivery stool, if it is a boy, kill him; but if it is a girl, let her live." [17] The midwives, however, feared God and did not do what the king of Egypt had told them to do; they let the boys live. [18] Then the king of Egypt summoned the midwives and asked them, "Why have you done this? Why have you let the boys live?" [19] The midwives answered Pharaoh, "Hebrew women are not like Egyptian women; they are vigorous and give birth before the midwives arrive." [20] So God was kind to the midwives and the people increased and became even more numerous. [21] And because the midwives feared God, he gave them families of their own. [22] Then Pharaoh gave this order to all his people: "Every boy that is born you must throw into the Nile, but let every girl live."

It would be incorrect to assume that Shiphrah and Puah were the only two midwives in Egypt. They were most likely high-ranking midwives (due to their Egyptian names), who served in Pharaoh's house, and were probably in charge of all the midwives in the land of Egypt. Shiphrah and Puah provide us another picture of leadership.

This might be a good place to introduce the concept that there are different levels of leadership. There are three levels of leadership:

Level 3
Leader of Leaders
Level 2
Influential Leadership
Level 1
Positional Leadership

LEVEL 1 LEADERSHIP = POSITIONAL LEADERSHIP.

Positional leadership is the lowest level of leadership. At level 1, you are a leader because of a certain job position or title you hold. At this level, people follow you because they feel they have to. Pharaoh clearly had positional leadership. He had the title and position of *"Pharaoh."*

It is important to recognize that you can have a *"position"* of leadership but not have people enthusiastically following you. Positional leadership could include being:

a) A member of a local church board voted into the position by members.
b) A member of a board for a denomination when selected by the assembly.
c) A pastor, newly called to a local church.

You can have a *"position"* of leadership but not have people following you enthusiastically. It is only as you build trust and confidence in people in your leadership that you achieve *"influence."* And a leader can lose his or her influence very quickly by breaking trust or demonstrating poor character.

LEVEL 2 LEADERSHIP = INFLUENTIAL LEADERSHIP.

To become more than *"the boss"* people follow only because they are required to, you must master the skills to invest in people and build trust. At this level a person may have an official title or not, but more importantly, you have built trust and have influence on a specific group of people. At this level, people follow you because they trust you and want to.

There is a huge difference between an authoritative boss and a trust-building leader. What's the difference? What does a boss do? A boss drives with authority. *"I'm the boss and this is the way it's going to be."* A boss drives with authority.

A level 2 leader inspires by trust. The currency of influence is always trust. Just because you have a position, or a title, does not mean that you have people's trust. In the Exodus story, Shiphrah and Puah illustrate influential, trust-building leadership.

LEVEL 3 LEADERSHIP = LEADER OF LEADERS. At level 3, the leader has influence over other leaders who, in turn, have influence over a specific group of people. At this level, you need to be able to help people develop their skills to become leaders and inspire people to their highest leadership potential. Over the coming chapters you and I are going to see how God developed Moses into a level three leader, a leader of leaders.

Let's return to our discussion of Shiphrah and Puah and the duties of these midwives. In Biblical times, midwives, rather than doctors, assisted women in giving birth. Midwives would have served the Egyptian, as well as, the large Hebrew population. But rather than helping with delivery, Shiphrah and Puah were ordered to kill all Hebrew male babies. Why male babies? The answer is obvious when you think about it. Females could be used as working slaves and presented no military threat. Boys, on the other hand, might become warriors!

It's hard for us to fully grasp the gravity of this situation. Puah and Shiphrah were slaves who stood before the most powerful man in the ancient world. Pharaoh's authority extended beyond reasonable measures. The wave of his hand could mean continued life or instant death! To these women, who at the time would have been viewed as lower than cattle in worth, Pharaoh ordered them to kill all Hebrew male babies at birth. Refusing to comply would mean their lives.

Most of us will not face life or death situations like Shiphrah and Puah faced. However, I think it safe to say that we all, at some point in our lives, will stand at crossroads where we will have a decision to make. Will we take the left road or the right? Will we follow the wide, easy road that most people want us to take or will we take the more difficult road that we know is the right road? Strong spiritual leadership begins with the courage to do the right thing, the thing God calls us to do. It is probably why Warren Bennis and Burt Nanus define a leader as someone who is *"doing the right thing,"* when doing the right thing is not always easy!

Do you remember the Apostle Paul's admonition to Christians living in Rome? He wrote to them: *"Do not be conformed to this world, but be transformed by the renewing of your mind, that you may prove what the will of God is, that which is good and acceptable and perfect"* (Romans 12:2). What was Paul saying? Choose the right road! If you take the wide road, you're conforming, being molded, being just like everyone else around you. You're fitting in!

If you are allowing the world to form you, then the world is leading your life, not God. A true leader operates on conviction and has courage of conviction. Martin Luther King Jr. once said, *"Most people are thermometers that record or register the temperature of majority opinion, not thermostats that transform and regulate the temperature of society."* A leader sets the standard.

Imagine how Shiphrah and Puah felt when the King called them in. You might think that they would feel intimidated. But they were not. In fact, the opposite: they turned aside the King's question with its veiled insult to the Egyptian women. Don't miss the irony here. Here is Pharaoh thinking he was going to deal shrewdly with these women, but it is these two midwives who end up dealing shrewdly with him.

So why did these two women refuse to obey the order of the Pharaoh? Well, verse 17 tells us: *"The midwives, however, feared God and did not do what the king of Egypt had told them to do; they let the boys live."* They refused to obey. Their courageous decision is consistent with the instruction of Acts 5:29 which says, *"We must obey God rather than men!"* Shiphrah and Puah made a much harder decision than any of us will, hopefully, ever have to make. But they made it because they feared God more than they feared Pharaoh and it would be God they obeyed! They feared displeasing God more than they feared displeasing people, so they obeyed God.

One of the common temptations for leaders is trying to please people. But people-pleasing will keep you from becoming the leader God designed you to be. To develop as a leader, you'll want to process your own need to please people. Why is it that you feel the need to please people? Ultimately, to develop as a leader you'll have to make a choice that became very clear for the Apostle Paul in his own leadership. *"Am I now trying to win the approval of men, or of God? Or am I trying to please men? If I were still trying to please men, I would not be a servant of Christ"* (Galatians 1:10).

EXERCISE: *Pleasing God or pleasing people*

Spend a few moments thinking about this and write down why you think leaders might become people-pleasers.

_____

_____

_____

_____

_____

_____

_____

We sometimes think that because we are not in a high-level leadership position or because we do not have a title, we cannot lead, or we cannot make any difference. In the minds of some, Shiphrah and Puah were *"nobodies."* They did not have a title like *"Pharaoh."* They didn't command an army like Pharaoh. They were nothing more than midwives.

Think about how they must have felt. The fear, the anxiety, the self-doubt. *"Who are we?"* They must have entertained thoughts like: *"What difference can we make? If we don't do it, someone else will. All we'll achieve is the anger of the Pharaoh. He'll probably have us put to death."*

Nevertheless, they did what was right. What courage Shiphrah and Puah demonstrated! Courage like this builds trust between the leader and followers and inspires. Their decision to do the right thing probably influenced many other midwives to do the same. The truth is positional leadership is the lowest level of leadership. You can have a position of leadership. You can have a title. But the actual test of whether you are leading or not is looking behind you to see if anyone is following. Shiphrah and Puah had incredible influence.

It was not long, however, before Pharaoh realized that the Hebrew babies were being allowed to live and so he called the two midwives in again for an explanation. Pharaoh asked them, *"Why have you done this? Why have you let the boys live?"* Shiphrah and Puah replied, *"Hebrew women are not like Egyptian women; they are vigorous and give birth before the midwives arrive."* Well, this may not have been the absolute truth!

Because of their courageous leadership, God blessed them and blessed all the midwives by prospering their families (as Exodus 1:21 says in some versions, *"giving them a large family"*). The text is not specific in terms of Puah and Shiphrah, but the midwives, in general, were blessed for their obedience.

Consider the leadership of Shiphrah and Puah for a moment. They used their personal influence for good and refused to follow the leadership of Pharaoh to kill the Hebrew male babies. Think about this! Without their courageous leadership, we would not have Moses.

What we are going to discover in our study of the book of Exodus is that God will choose an unlikely leader—Moses—to lead the people of Israel out of bondage on a journey to the Promise Land. Over the next thirteen chapters, we will be looking closely at Moses as a model of transformational leadership to learn how we can better lead change in a change-saturated world.

EXPOSURE: The leadership of Moses

Perhaps it is hard for you to think of yourself as a leader. But take a look at the real Moses! What is quite *interesting*, and what I want to get you thinking about in this first chapter, is that Moses was a very unlikely leader.

When most of us hear the name *"Moses,"* the award-winning film *The Ten Commandments*, directed by the great Cecil B. DeMille, comes to mind. The image of the famous actor, Charlton Heston, is indelibly etched in our minds. In his role as Moses, Heston portrayed a vibrant, strong, handsome and confident Moses.

For the younger generation with young children, you probably have watched the movie *The Prince of Egypt*. This Prince of Egypt version of Moses presents us with a high energy, fun-loving, and ageless version of the leader of the Hebrews. But think for a moment. Both the Moses of *The Ten Commandments* and *The Prince of Egypt* are Hollywood's version.

In the real story of Moses' life that comes to us from the book of Exodus, Moses is described in very human terms: with all his self-doubts, his disappointments, his struggle to balance family with his role as leader and the many challenges he faced. One reason why Moses is so accessible to us is that his life is much like ours.

The resume of the real Moses reveals . . .

- **Not in his prime—80 years of age.** He's not the guy you would typically interview and hire for the job of leading the Hebrews out of bondage toward the Promise Land. You'd always have the thought, *"Is this guy even going to make it to Promise Land?"*
- **Very reluctant.** Moses lacked confidence and was riddled with insecurity.
- **Not the most gifted.** Not a great communicator. Not a quick-minded strategist. Not the most charismatic person you've ever met.
- **Anger issues.** Moses had issues, specifically a serious anger issue. He lacked self-control with respect to anger and often blurted out the inappropriate or worse, taking a swing at someone. Speaking of taking a swing at someone, we'll learn, in the next chapter, that Moses was a . . .
- **Murderer.** That's right. He took the life of another human being. It's the kind of thing you don't overlook when you are reviewing someone's resume who is applying for a high-level leadership position.

But reading your Bible, you'll discover that God has always chosen the most unlikely leaders to accomplish His purposes. Jacob cheated, Peter had a temper, David had an affair, Noah got drunk, Jonah ran from God, Gideon was insecure, Miriam gossiped, Martha worried, Thomas doubted, Sara was impatient, Elijah was moody, Zacchaeus was short, Abraham was old and Lazarus was dead.

Here's my point: If God can use a Moses . . . why can't God use you?

EXPOSURE: *Leadership Styles*

The range of leadership roles and styles assumed by Moses during his life reflect his flexibility. He was able to adapt his style to the various needs of the people and the various situations they faced.

Different situations and different people call for different leadership styles. Bill Hybels, in his book, *Courageous Leadership*, identifies ten styles of leadership for our consideration. As you read this next section, I would challenge you to try to identify your leadership styles. Try to identify three or four styles that you have employed or are inclined to try. Here then are ten leadership styles:

1. **THE VISIONARY LEADERSHIP STYLE.** What distinguishes the visionary leader is that he or she operates from a clear picture of what the future could hold. Visionary leaders love to cast clear and compelling vision and exhibit incredible passion around turning vision into reality.
2. **THE DIRECTIONAL LEADERSHIP STYLE.** The focus and strength of this kind of leader is their discerning ability to choose the right path for an organization as it approaches a critical intersection.
3. **THE STRATEGIC LEADERSHIP STYLE.** Leaders employing this style have the God-given ability to take an existing vision and break it down into a series of sequential,

achievable steps. The gifting of this kind of leadership provides a congregation the specific steps to take in order to march towards the vision.

4. **THE MANAGING LEADERSHIP STYLE.** Some leadership literature draws a hard line between leaders and managers. They'll say something like, "Leaders do the right things, while managers do things right." While the distinction is helpful to gain clarity about leadership, the person with a managing leadership style has the God-given ability to organize people, resources, and processes to achieve the mission.

5. **THE MOTIVATIONAL LEADERSHIP STYLE.** These persons have the God-given ability to keep their teammates fired up. They are encouragers and affirmers, and while some view motivational leadership as a lightweight style of leadership, this style of leadership is indispensable, especially when the journey towards the vision gets hard or the journey is long.

6. **THE SHEPHERDING LEADERSHIP STYLE.** Persons with this style slowly build a community and team by loving, nurturing, and gently supporting members of the community. This kind of leadership moves people toward the vision by their care. John Maxwell is fond of saying, *"people do not care how much you know, until they know how much you care."*

7. **THE TEAM-BUILDING LEADERSHIP STYLE.** Team-builders have a gifting that allows them to successfully find and develop the right people with the right abilities, the right character, and the right chemistry to serve with other team members. They love teams. The difference between the shepherding style and this style is that the former's focus is people, whereas the team-builder's focus is the cause or the mission.

8. **THE ENTREPRENEURAL LEADERSHIP STYLE.** Persons employing this style may possess any of the other leadership styles, but what distinguishes these leaders is that they function optimally in start-up situations. These kinds of leaders are highly creative and have a bias towards *"the new"*—as

in new ministries or new churches. Church planters are a perfect example of the entrepreneurial leader.

9. **THE REENGINEERING LEADERSHIP STYLE.** These leaders are at their best in environments needing a turn-around or renewal. When churches lose their way, get off mission, or become stagnate, engineering leaders thrive in helping these kinds of churches find their way back on mission or regain their passion.

10. **THE BRIDGE-BUILDING LEADERSHIP STYLE.** Leaders with this style have the unique ability to bring together, under a single leadership umbrella, a wide range of constituencies. Think of these kinds of leaders as spiritual diplomats who have the God-given wisdom and ability to appropriately compromise and negotiate in order to get everyone on the same page.

EXERCISE: *Your leadership styles*

After you've identified three or four styles that you have employed or have been inclined to try, in a small group with other leaders, have everyone share their three or four styles and provide examples. Also share what you think is the value of knowing your style.

1. _____
2. _____
3. _____
4. _____

EXPERIENCE: *Leadership definitions*

Post a variety of the leadership definitions from this chapter around the room. Have participants stand by one that speaks to them or shows their leadership values. Have them explain why they chose the definition they did, why it is relevant to them.

Chapter 2

GOD'S SHAPING OF A LEADER

Exodus 2

KEY PRINCIPLE: GOD SHAPES A LEADER OVER A LIFETIME THROUGH DEFINING MOMENTS AND PIVOTAL PEOPLE.

"God develops leaders over a lifetime."
—J. Robert Clinton, *The Making of a Leader*

EXPOSURE: *Life-defining experiences*

One early evening when I was four years old, my parents drove my sister and me to our grandparents' home. I loved visiting my grandparents; so, when the car pulled to the curb I quickly leaped out and took off across the street. But as I hurried out into the street, beyond the reach of my parents, an oncoming car turned the corner and struck me. I suffered a serious head injury and was taken to the hospital where I remained for weeks. I can remember only a little of my hospital stay, but that experience was life-defining for me.

I grew up being told countless times, especially by my grandmother, that I was alive because of a miracle, that I was alive because everyone in the church had been praying for me. I grew up with the thought, that God had saved me for a purpose, indelibly etched in my consciousness. This experience was defining for me.

There are moments in all our lives that are life-defining. I call them *defining moments*. These defining moments are like landmarks on a road map. These moments mark key points along your life's journey. Defining moments are like game-changers in a football game, in that they change the direction of the game. God uses such defining moments to shape us as leaders!

A defining moment occurs when you come face-to-face with a truth, a truth that confronts you to change the way you live. It demands a decision, and regardless of the choice you make, you are never the same. We are all shaped by defining moments, and God uses these defining moments to shape us as leaders.

You've probably heard it said that *"God does not call the qualified; God qualifies the called."* What exactly does that mean? What we're going to learn, in this chapter of our study of Moses, is that God qualifies and shapes a person for leadership over a lifetime through what I call *"defining moments."* J. Robert Clinton, in his little book, The Making of a Leader, calls them *"critical incidents."* He writes:

"God develops leaders over a lifetime. That development is a function of the use of events and people to impress leadership lessons upon a leader . . . All leaders can point to critical incidents in their lives where God taught them something very important." (p 25)

EXERCISE: Defining moments

God has been shaping you over a lifetime to be a person of influence, to be a leader. He has been using defining moments to accomplish this shaping. Can you identify three defining moments in your life?

- _____
  _____
  _____
  _____
  _____

- _____
  _____
  _____
  _____
  _____
  _____

- _____
  _____
  _____
  _____
  _____
  _____

Let's look at Moses, in Exodus 2, to see how God shaped him for future leadership. We are actually going to look at three of Moses' defining moments beginning with his miraculous deliverance from death.

- **First Defining Moment: Moses' Miraculous Deliverance**

Exodus 2:1-10

¹ Now a man of the house of Levi married a Levite woman, ² and she became pregnant and gave birth to a son. When she saw that he was a fine child, she hid him for three months. ³ But when she could hide him no longer, she got a papyrus basket for him and coated it with tar and pitch. Then she placed the child in it and put it among the reeds along the bank of the Nile. ⁴ His sister stood at a distance to see what would happen to him. ⁵ Then Pharaoh's daughter went down to the Nile to bathe, and her attendants were walking along the riverbank. She saw the basket among the reeds and sent her slave girl to get it. ⁶ She opened it and saw the baby. He was crying, and she felt sorry for him. "This is one of the Hebrew babies," she said. ⁷ Then his sister asked Pharaoh's daughter, "Shall I go and get one of the Hebrew women to nurse the baby for you?" ⁸ "Yes, go," she answered. And the girl went and got the baby's mother. ⁹ Pharaoh's daughter said to her, "Take this baby and nurse him for me, and I will pay you." So, the woman took the baby and nursed him. ¹⁰ When the child grew older, she took him to Pharaoh's daughter, and he became her son. She named him Moses, saying, "I drew him out of the water."

Moses' miraculous deliverance from death as a baby was defining. Moses could have been among the many babies killed because of Pharaoh's decree. But he escaped death and was given the name Moses. His name literally means *"drawn out,"* and is indicative of his future role. Moses will eventually, not just draw his people out of slavery, but also draw them through the waters of the Dead Sea on their journey toward Mount Sinai and the Promise Land.

Moses would have been reminded many times of how he had been delivered. How do you think this would have shaped Moses' understanding of God and his purpose? Do you think he entertained the idea that God saved him for a purpose?

I ask these questions because it is important to not only identify your defining moments, but also to process them. How do you process a defining moment? Here are three process questions that invite personal reflection by essentially asking, *"What could God have been up to in allowing this defining moment in my life?"*

- How did this moment shape me?
- How did I come away from this experience different than I was before the experience?
- What ideas, beliefs or values do I now hold as a result of having been through that experience?

Consider Moses' defining moment of miraculously being saved as a baby. What could God have been up to in allowing this defining moment in Moses' life? Had he been *"drawn out"* so that later he could draw his people out of slavery? Had he been delivered to serve as a delivering leader? Perhaps Moses grew up believing that God had saved him for a purpose. Perhaps Moses grew up with a strong confidence in God to miraculously deliver people who take courageous action in faith.

Reggie McNeal makes this insightful comment about Moses: "Yahweh made sure that Moses, the future deliverer, would grow up with the knowledge that he himself had been delivered through divine intervention." (*A Work of Heart*, p. 4-5) The future deliverer had been miraculously delivered himself! What an important life lesson for him!

Now, let's consider a second defining moment in Moses' life, when he had an altercation with an Egyptian slave master.

- **Second Defining Moment: Moses' Altercation with the Egyptian Slave Master**

Exodus 2:11-15

11 One day, after Moses had grown up, he went out to where his own people were and watched them at their hard labor. He saw an Egyptian beating a Hebrew, one of his own people. 12 Glancing this way and that and seeing no one, he killed the Egyptian and hid him in the sand. 13 The next day he went out and saw two Hebrews fighting. He asked the one in the wrong, "Why are you hitting your fellow Hebrew?" 14 The man said, "Who made you ruler and judge over us? Are you thinking of killing me as you killed the Egyptian?" Then Moses was afraid and thought, "What I did must have become known." 15 When Pharaoh heard of this, he tried to kill Moses, but Moses fled from Pharaoh and went to live in Midian, where he sat down by a well.

What this story highlights is that not all defining moments are positive. The truth is, we can be shaped and defined as much or more by a negative defining moment as we can a positive defining moment.

Sheri is an extraordinary leader in the social work field. She brings incredible passion for justice, inexhaustible energy and a never-say-die, can-do approach to addressing real life challenges. But Sheri would tell you that one of her most significant defining moments was when she was a child. When she was five years old her father died suddenly. Her mother had to work two jobs in order to pay the bills and provide food for her and her two brothers. Seeing how challenging it was for her mother as a single woman shaped her to want to help others. Would she want to go through anything like it again? No! But is she thankful for how that experience shaped her life? Absolutely!

Consider that Moses was the product of two worlds. Reggie McNeal observes about Moses that *"He was a child of two cultures, who never completely belonged to either."* (*A Work of Heart,* p. 7) Moses grew up exposed to great affluence being raised in Pharaoh's palace. But he also grew up seeing his own people, the Hebrews, abused by a system of slavery imposed by Pharaoh. This experience clearly shaped Moses to be the leader he became, a leader with a strong sense of, and passion for, justice.

Moses was born to a Hebrew mother and nursed by her in his early years at the request of the Egyptian princess, who knew that he was a Hebrew. When he had grown sufficiently, which means that he was weaned, he was brought to the palace, where he matured in the context of Egyptian power and culture. In this palace environment, Moses was exposed to Egyptian models of authority and leadership. *"The irony, of course, is that the very knowledge and skills he learns in Pharaoh's house will be used in his confrontation with Pharaoh upon his return to Egypt later on."* (Norman J. Cohen, *Moses and the Journey to Leader*, p. 8)

One day, leaving the place of his youth, Moses goes out to his kinsfolk, his own people. What seems to drive Moses is an intense desire to connect with his brother and sisters. Exodus 2:11 describes the day Moses went out this way: *"One day, after Moses had grown up, he went out to where his own people were and watched them at their hard labor. He saw an Egyptian beating a Hebrew, one of his own people."*

He left the comfort of the palace to see his own people, and in doing so his life was dramatically changed. Sometimes, an individual who aspires to leadership must be willing to give up the comfort zone, the easier lifestyle, in order to serve the community. And frequently there is little to gain and much to lose. Moses, in becoming involved with Hebrew slaves, had everything to lose.

Moses was not blind to the wealth and power of his surroundings. He was able to see the enslaved Hebrew as brothers and sisters, a point brought out by a repetition of the words *"his own people."* He saw their burdens. He saw the injustice. He saw an Egyptian beating a Hebrew and he acted. Exodus 2:12 says, *"Looking this way and that and seeing no one, he killed the Egyptian and hid him in the sand."* Moses intervened and it became a defining moment in his life.

Though Moses feared being caught, as evidenced by his turning from side to side to ensure that no one was watching, he nevertheless was willing to risk everything to save a fellow Israelite. Moses demonstrated, even at this early stage in his development, a willingness to act out of a sense of justice, doing what is right no matter what the cost. What caused him to insert himself in the situation is a very strong sense of justice.

The text emphasizes that Moses went out twice, two days in a row. *"The next day he went out and saw two Hebrews fighting. He asked the one in the wrong, "Why are you hitting your fellow Hebrew?"* (Exodus 2:13) Note that Moses' sense of justice did not hinge only on whether it affected only his own people. Moses stood on principle, on values, even when it involved his own people.

Moses exhibited here one of the crucial qualities of a leader: the ability to discern the nature of circumstances and to know what to do. According to Leith Anderson, *"Leadership is figuring out what needs to be done and then doing it."* Figure what the right thing to do is and then do it!

Just don't expect people to be always happy with you doing what needs to be done. One of the Hebrews turned to Moses and asked, *"Who made you ruler and judge over us? Are you thinking of killing me as you killed the Egyptian?"* Young leaders are often challenged because of their perceived youth and lack of experience, and at times this criticism is a difficult hurdle to overcome. Like Moses, we all carry much personal baggage as we assume leadership positions, and we too face the challenge of carrying that baggage with us into our new roles.

Having acted on his principles, his values, having put himself on the line, Moses was forced to flee to the desert. He was forced to give up the comforts of life in Pharaoh's palace.

This defining moment clarifies that even righteous anger, without self-control, can be dangerous and destructive. Like all of us, Moses had his issues and one of his issues was his anger. This is not to say that all anger is wrong. Righteous anger towards injustice is not wrong at all. But Moses always had difficulty keeping his anger *"in check"* and under control. Throughout his life, God would provide Moses many opportunities to learn this lesson, though it appears that Moses fought his battle with anger all his life.

There is an important leader-shaping principle that I want to introduce here. It is the **"Follow, Then Lead"** Principle. Great leaders know the importance of great following. One of the important lessons that God will teach every spiritual leader is obedience to God as our ultimate Leader.

All of us have an idea of what it means to lead and what it means to follow from a game we learned as children. Do you remember the childhood game called "Follow the Leader" where the leader would do certain motions, and everybody would follow whatever the leader said or did?

Well, in the church we say that Jesus is our Leader. However, we don't always follow Jesus though we claim Him as our Leader. In the church, many think it enough to study what Jesus said, and we consider ourselves spiritual if we memorize what Jesus said. Some of us even pride ourselves in knowing what Jesus said in Greek, the original language of the New Testament. But the real point is this: are we actually following our Leader? Are we doing what Jesus called us to do?

One of the keys of being a person of influence, a great spiritual leader is being a good follower. People are influenced by spiritual leaders who follow the Leader. Research indicates that people look for credibility, trustworthiness and integrity more than anything else in a leader they would think about following.

A third defining moment for Moses was the time he escaped to Midian and spent years shepherding his future father-in-law's sheep.

- **Third Defining Moment: Moses' Desert Experience**

Exodus 2:15-25

15 When Pharaoh heard of this, he tried to kill Moses, but Moses fled from Pharaoh and went to live in Midian, where he sat down by a well. 16 Now a priest of Midian had seven daughters, and they came to draw water and fill the troughs to water their father's flock. 17 Some shepherds came along and drove them away, but Moses got up and came to their rescue and watered their flock. 18 When the girls returned to Reuel their father, he asked them, "Why have you returned so early today?" 19 They answered, "An Egyptian rescued us from the shepherds. He even drew water for us and watered the flock." 20 "And where is he?" he asked his daughters. "Why did you leave him? Invite him to have something to eat." 21 Moses agreed to stay with the man, who gave his daughter Zipporah to Moses in marriage. 22 Zipporah gave birth to a son, and Moses named him Gershom, saying, "I have become an alien in a foreign land." 23 During that long period, the king of Egypt died. The Israelites groaned in their slavery and cried out, and their cry for help because of their slavery went up to God. 24 God heard their groaning and he remembered his covenant with Abraham, with Isaac and with Jacob. 25 So God looked on the Israelites and was concerned about them.

Moses fled Egypt and went to live in Midian. When he arrived at a well, he witnessed a group of shepherds driving off the daughters of Reuel, (more commonly known as Jethro), who had come to water their father's flock. Moses rose to their defense. Once again, Moses' sense of justice moved him to act, illustrating that a leader's values ultimately get reflected in what he or she chooses to do.

The text literally says Moses redeemed them (va-yoshian) and watered their flock. This odd choice of words speaks of the role he is destined to play on behalf of his own people one day: He will redeem them from Egypt. (Norman J. Cohen, *Moses and the Journey to Leadership*, p. 13)

Moses' Midian desert experience became another defining moment. In the Midian desert Moses continued to develop his capacity for leadership as he tended sheep. Reggie McNeil comments:

> *"Shepherding leadership differed significantly from the Egyptian style of leadership that Moses had been taught, a method of authoritarian power and whiplash persuasion employed by taskmasters, princes and Pharaohs. The desert school of leadership built accountability and stewardship into Moses' character. He tended someone else's flock. He was responsible for his father-in-law's assets. He had to demonstrate not only trustworthiness but also resourcefulness to ensure the sustainability of the flock. Moses' Exodus leadership would draw from these wilderness lessons. He would attend another's flock, assuming responsibility for food, water, safety, and flock perpetuity. These commonplace activities of shepherds shaped Moses' heart into the heart of a shepherd leader."* (McNeil, A Work of Heart, p. 11)

Having left behind the shelter and comfort of Pharaoh's palace, and having become the shepherd of Jethro's flock, Moses further honed the skills he would need to lead people through the desert to the land of Canaan. As Moses drove Jethro's sheep into the wilderness, caring for each animal and leading them to water, so, too, Moses would lead the people of Israel through the desert for forty years. Dr. Norman J. Cohen writes:

> *"Throughout the literature of the Ancient Near East and later, the role of shepherd symbolizes leadership. People are often compared to a flock or a herd, and shepherding is considered a training ground for those destined to lead. There are numerous references*

in the Bible to leaders who were shepherds in their earlier lives;
for example, King David. The Rabbis stress that Moses gains
the necessary experience to redeem Israel and lead the people to
the Promised Land precisely because he had been leading Jethro's
flock in the wilderness." (Cohen, *Moses and the Journey to*
Leadership, p. 16)

It is in the Midian desert that Moses developed into a *shepherd leader* as
he continued to grow and mature. In Median, in contrast to his time in
Egypt, he exercised more restraint and the result was markedly different.
Here he didn't act like a violent vigilante, but rather a compassionate,
caring shepherd.

Here in the desert, Moses was estranged from his former life, but
found some sense of connection with Jethro's family, marrying Jethro's
daughter Zipporah. Yet, we know nothing about these years away from
his people except for the description of him shepherding his father-in-
law's flock. Leaders develop personal characteristics and skills over time;
it takes a series of experiences, each one building on the others, to ensure
growth. Leadership is not born overnight. Leadership development
takes times.

EXERCISE: *Processing your defining moments*

With each of your three defining moments, answer the three processing
questions: How did this moment shape me? How did I come away from
this experience different than I was before the experience? What ideas,
beliefs or values do I now hold as a result of having been through that
experience?

- _____
  _____
  _____

_____

_____

• _____

_____

_____

_____

_____

• _____

_____

_____

_____

_____

EXPOSURE: Pivotal people

God not only uses defining moments to shape us, God also uses what I call *"pivotal people."* My grandmother was one the most spiritually influential persons in my life. When I was in elementary school, my grandmother came to live next door. I remember visiting her most afternoons after school. I remember enjoying her great chicken noodle soup. She was one of those persons who often reminded me after the automobile accident that God had saved my life for a purpose. My grandmother was a praying grandmother, who prayed every day for me. She was one of the persons God used to cast the vision for me to become a pastor, reminding me that God had miraculously saved me following the automobile accident.

There are pivotal people in all our lives whom God uses to shape us. Again, in the book, *The Making of a Leader*, J. Robert Clinton, referring to them as *"divine contacts,"* writes:

"A divine contact [or a "pivotal person"] is the person whom God brings a leader at a crucial moment in a development phase in order to affirm leadership potential, to encourage leadership potential, to give guidance on a special issue, to give insights that broaden the leader, to challenge the leader toward God, or to open a door to ministry opportunity." (p 129)

In Moses' life, his Hebrew mother and adopting Egyptian mother were certainly pivotal persons for his spiritual development and shaping. Their courageous leadership in doing the difficult, hard thing would shape his understanding of what is required of a leader.

Later in his life, Moses' father-in-law, Jethro became a pivotal person in Moses' leadership shaping. Jethro served as a father figure for Moses. In Jethro, Moses found blessing, encouragement, guidance and counsel that shaped Moses in his development as a leader.

"Cut off from his natural father at an early age, and significantly distanced from his adoptive father, Moses needed a father figure to make the transition from leader 'wanna-be' to real leader of God's people." (Reggie McNeal, *A Work of Heart*, p. 9)

In the desert school of leadership, Moses learned the **"Little, Then Much"** principle which Jesus introduced to His disciples. Jesus said, *"Whoever can be trusted with very little can also be trusted with much, and whoever is dishonest with very little will also be dishonest with much."* (Luke 16:10) The *"Little, Then Much"* principle is the concept that God often provides us little opportunities to lead before God provides us greater opportunities.

You may not appreciate the importance of small tasks now, but successfully accomplishing smaller tasks prepares you for larger tasks that God is quite willing to give you in time. If you do not take seriously the smaller tasks that God puts before you, God will not provide greater opportunities. What you'll find is that God will provide you the same lesson over again until you learn the importance of being faithful in the little things.

> *"If you think serving others is below you . . .*
> *then leadership is too far above you!"*

This principle is reflected in the qualifications for elders in the church. First Timothy 3:4-6 describes someone being considered for eldership: "He must manage his own family well and see that his children obey him with proper respect. (If anyone does not know how to manage his own family, how can he take care of God's church?)" The principle is as simple as this: If you can't lead your family, how can you imagine leading the larger family of God?

So, let me ask, *"How do you handle the little tasks in your life?"* Do you take those tasks seriously? Do you handle them well? As you are faithful in leading in small ways, God will—in His time—provide you greater opportunities to lead!

EXERCISE: "Little, Then Much" principle

Identify and reflect on one of your more challenging *"little tasks"* and write down why you find this task a challenge.

_____

_____

_____

_____

_____

_____

_____

_____

_____

EXERCISE: *Defining pivotal persons*

God has been shaping you over a lifetime to be a person of influence, to be a leader. He has been using pivotal persons to accomplish this shaping. Can you identify three pivotal persons in your life that God has used to shape you?

- _____
  _____
  _____
  _____
  _____

- _____
  _____
  _____
  _____
  _____

- _____
  _____
  _____
  _____
  _____

Now, with respect to pivotal persons, let me give you three process questions. We process the impact and influence of pivotal persons in our lives by asking questions like:

- How did this person encourage you toward leadership?
- What did I learn from this individual?
- What values or beliefs do I hold that more than likely were influenced by this person?

EXERCISE: *Processing your pivotal persons*

- _____
  _____
  _____
  _____
  _____

- _____
  _____
  _____
  _____
  _____

- _____
  _____
  _____
  _____
  _____

As you conclude this chapter, take a moment to pray. Ask God to continue His shaping work in your life so that you can become the person God wants you to be. Ask God to reveal to you how you can be a person of greater influence, a more effective leader.

EXPERIENCE: *Tallest Tower*

For this experience you will need a variety of items to build the tallest tower. The items can be anything readily available such as: toothpicks, newspaper, wooden blocks, tape, books, cards, pop cans, uncooked pasta, etc. If you have a large number of participants, you could have two of more teams, but keep the items similar for each team. The goal is to build the tallest, freestanding structure from the provided items in an allotted amount of time (perhaps 5-8 minutes). This is an ideal activity for creative problem-solving and improving collaboration. Follow-up process questions could include:

1. Who came up with the design?
2. Who was the leader?
3. What observations do you have about collaboration?
4. Why was your team successful or not successful?

CHAPTER 3

THE POWER OF VISION

Exodus 3:1-10

KEY PRINCIPLE: GOD GIVES VISION TO A LEADER AND TEAM TO INSPIRE PEOPLE TO WANT TO CHANGE.

"Where there is no vision, the people perish."
—Proverbs 29:18, KJV

EXPOSURE: Moses' encounter with God and God's vision for Moses

God's call to Moses to lead came in the form of a literal *"burning bush"* experience when he was eighty years old. Eighty years of age! Apparently, we are never too old to exert influence; never too old to lead.

Dwight L. Moody described the life of Moses this way:

> *"Moses spent his first forty years thinking he was somebody. He spent his second forty years learning he was a nobody. He spent his third forty years discovering what God can do with a nobody."* (*What the Bible Is All About*, Henrietta C. Mears, Ventura, CA: Gospel Light Publications, 1966, p.33)

Read about Moses' *"burning bush"* experience.

> **Exodus 3:1-6**
>
> *¹ Now Moses was tending the flock of Jethro his father-in-law, the priest of Midian, and he led the flock to the far side of the desert and came to Horeb, the mountain of God. ² There the angel of the LORD appeared to him in flames of fire from within a bush. Moses saw that though the bush was on fire it did not burn up. ³ So Moses thought, "I will go over and see this strange sight—why the bush does not burn up." ⁴ When the LORD saw that he had gone over to look, God called to him from within the bush, "Moses! Moses!" And Moses said, "Here I am." ⁵ "Do not come any closer," God said. "Take off your sandals, for the place where you are standing is holy ground." ⁶ Then he said, "I am the God of your father, the God of Abraham, the God of Isaac and the God of Jacob." At this, Moses hid his face, because he was afraid to look at God.*

Moses encountered God in the lowliest of trees God created, a bush. The Hebrew word names it as a *"thorny shrub."* Talk about God's unusual ways! God descends on the Mount of Horeb and manifests Himself in the most insignificant thorny bush in the desert. It was just a bush, like countless other bushes dotting the landscape of the Midian desert.

At first glance, this bush wasn't different or distinctive; but what was happening to this bush certainly distinguished it. Over the years of shepherding sheep in the Midian desert, Moses may have seen a bush or two catch fire, perhaps because of a lightning strike. The dry thorny bush would ignite and in a matter of minutes the bush would be consumed. But not this bush! This bush was inextinguishable. This bush was not consumed by the fire and Moses' eyes locked on it.

In seeing the burning bush, Moses marveled and was frightened at the same time. Curiosity motivated him to take a closer look. Upon moving closer, Moses heard a voice say, *"I am the God of your father, the God of Abraham, the God of Isaac and the God of Jacob."* (Exodus 3:6) Hearing this, Moses was afraid and hid his face from God.

This is another one of these defining moments when God gets our full and undivided attention for the purpose of giving us direction. God's direction is sometimes given through what is called *"vision."* One of the ways that God gives direction to a leader is through a vision of what God wants to accomplish.

Moses is a model of a visionary leader. God's very specific call on Moses' life, God's vision for Moses, came like this:

Exodus 3:7-10

"I have indeed seen the misery of my people in Egypt. I have heard them crying out because of their slave drivers, and I am concerned about their suffering. ⁸ So I have come down to rescue them from the hand of the Egyptians and to bring them up out of that land into a good and spacious land, a land flowing with milk and honey—the home of the Canaanites, Hittites, Amorites, Perizzites, Hivites and Jebusites. ⁹ And now the cry of the Israelites has reached me, and I have seen the way the Egyptians are oppressing them. ¹⁰ So now, go. I am sending you to Pharaoh to bring my people the Israelites out of Egypt."

God informed Moses, *"You, Moses, think you are the only one who hears and is affected by the people's cries? I, too, hear them and will rescue them."* God wanted Moses to know that He not only was witnessing Israel's suffering, God was actually suffering along with the people. The prophet Isaiah said of God, *"In all their distress he too was distressed."* (Isaiah 63:9) Vision is often birthed out of unfavorable, even painful, conditions.

The vision that Moses is asked to convey spotlights God as the Deliverer, the One who will free the people. Eric Fromm speaks of two kinds of freedom: *"freedom from"* and *"freedom to."* The vison that God gives Moses includes both components. God will bring them out—out from under the yoke of the Egyptians. And God will bring them to— a land into a good and spacious land, a land flowing with milk and honey.

Like Moses, every leader has the challenge to formulate and communicate a clear and compelling vision of the group's future. The vision ought to include an articulation of what the group will move from and what the group will move toward. Nothing is more important than this for a leader, and how well it is accomplished will determine the leader's ultimate success or failure.

EXERCISE: God's vision for Moses

In reading the verses above, God describes where He is inviting Moses to lead the people. Close your eyes and use your imagination to describe the place Moses would be leading the people of Israel and how that place would be different from where they presently lived. Describe the destination in your own words.

_____

_____

_____

_____

_____

_____

_____

EXPOSURE: What is vision?

Here are a couple of definitions of vision that will help you better understand what vision is. Richard Beckhard & Wendy Pritchard, in their book *Changing the Essence*, define vision this way:

> *"A vision is a picture of a future state for the organization, a description of what it would look like a number of years from now. It is a dynamic picture of the organization in the future, as seen by its leadership."*

George Barna, writes:

"Vision for ministry is a clear mental image of a preferable future imparted by God to His chosen servants and is based on an accurate understanding of God, self, and circumstances." (*The Power of Vision*)

With these two definitions in mind, here are the **ESSENTIAL COMPONENTS OF VISION:**

- **A vision is a clear mental picture.** Leaders with vision have a clear picture in their minds of where they are heading. Spiritual leaders have a clear mental picture of where God wants them to lead, and what sets leaders apart is that they see where God wants them to lead the group before others see it.

When Disney World, the famous amusement park, first opened, Mrs. Walt Disney was asked to speak at the Grand Opening, since Walt had died. She was introduced by a man who said, "Mrs. Disney, I just wish Walt could have seen this." She stood up and said, "He did," and sat down. Walt Disney had a vision for Disney World and that is why there is a Disney World.

The Reverend Dr. Martin Luther King, Jr., an American Baptist pastor, had a vision for America. He shared his vision on August 28, 1963, in Washington, D.C. on the steps of the Lincoln Memorial.

"I have a dream that my four little children will one day live in a nation where they will not be judged by the color of their skin but by the content of their character. I have a dream today! I have a dream that one day, down in Alabama, with its vicious racists, with its governor having his lips dripping with the words of "interposition" and "nullification"—one day right there in Alabama little black boys and black girls will be able to join hands with little white boys and white girls as sisters and brothers."

- **A vision is a picture of a preferable change.** A vision is a picture that involves change from the present condition. It is a preferred change or a change for the better. Albert Einstein said, *"Insanity is when you do the same thing over and over and expect a different result."* A vision implies change from how things are to how things could be. Change is such a critical part of vision that we will spend considerable time looking at leading change later.

- **A vision is a picture with a future focus.** Visionary leaders are always looking forward, not looking back. They are future-oriented. The higher you go in leadership, the more your work is about the future. Effective leaders work hard at gaining a clear picture of what they want to accomplish in the future. Vision is the foresight of a leader.

Robert K. Greenleaf, in his book *The Servant as Leader*, writes:

> *"Foresight is the 'lead' that the leader has. Once he loses this lead and events start to force his hand, he is leader in name only. He is not leading; he is reacting to immediate events and he probably will not long to be a leader. There are abundant current examples of loss of leadership which stem from a failure to foresee what reasonably could have been foreseen, and from failure to act on that knowledge while the leader has freedom to act."*

- **A vision is a picture imparted by God.** While it is quite common to speak of *"the vision of the leader,"* vision for spiritual leaders is really God's vision which God imparts to a leader for the purpose of providing clear direction toward a preferred future. Vision is God's gift to a leader and the community. We do not manufacture vision, but rather receive the vision God has for us and the community we are leading.

A vision is conceived in the heart of God and given birth in us when our hearts ache for the things that break God's heart. *"The Lord said,*

'I have indeed seen the misery of my people in Egypt. I have heard them crying out because of their slave drivers, and I am concerned about their suffering." (Exodus 3:7)

A vision provided by God will often cause an overwhelming sense of inadequacy and therefore will call for faith. We will look at the typical human response to God's vision and the need for courageous leadership in the next chapter, *The Calling of a Leader.*

EXPOSURE: What is the value of a God-given vision?

- **Vision clarifies our direction.** Vision answers the WHERE? question. Where are we going as a congregation or as a team? Stephen Covey writes, *"We are more in need of a vision or destination and a compass (a set of principles or directions) and less in need of a road map."* (Stephen Covey, *The Seven Habits of Highly Effective People*) Vision provides direction for the leader and the congregation.

- **Vision energizes us.** Burt Nanus says, *"There is no more powerful engine driving an organization toward excellence and long-range success than an attractive, worthwhile, and achievable vision of the future, widely shared."* (Burt Nanus, *Visionary Leadership*)

In his book, *Courageous Leadership*, Bill Hybels writes:

> *"Vision is at the core of leadership. It's the fire that creates action. It's the energy that creates passion . . . It's a picture of the future that produces passion in you."*

Vision energizes the leader, the congregation, and the team.

- **Vision focuses our energy.** Management consultant Peter Drucker says, *"No other principle of effectiveness is more violated today than the basic principle of concentration . . . . Our motto seems to be, 'Let's do a little bit of everything.'"*

I've often said that leading a congregation can be as challenging as trying to herd a bunch of cats. What vision does is it helps the leader to narrow the focus for the congregation or the team.

- **Vision unifies our team.** A shared vision helps everyone understand where we are heading. When everyone understands where we are going and buys into it, there is unity. Nothing unifies a team like a common and shared vision.

EXPOSURE: How do you receive God's vision?

I am often asked, *"How do you receive a vision for leading?"* First, let me be clear about where you don't find God's vision. You don't find God's vision in a book. You do not borrow one from another church or organization. No other leader can give you a vision for your church or organization. In this section I want to provide a practical process for you receiving God's unique vision for your congregation. One of the best resources I have found on vision is Will Mancini's book, *Church Unique*, from which I have relied heavily on in this section.

Vision is a mental picture of where God is leading. I've found it helpful to think of vision as a puzzle with many pieces that have to be put together. There are three key pieces that provide a beginning perspective of vision for a congregation: context, gifting, and passion. Let's look at these three pieces of the vision puzzle more closely.

CONTEXT involves the unique needs, challenges and opportunities where God has placed your church. God has placed you as a leader and your congregation in a specific place and time. Every place has unique needs, challenges and opportunities that distinguishes it from other places. *"By connecting the dots with the past, we bring new meaning to the present and walk into the future with a stronger sense of identity."* (Will Mancini, *Church Unique*) Here are some questions that can help you and your leadership team explore your context, the place where God would have you pursue His vision for you.

- What are the unique needs where God has placed us in our city or our neighborhood?
- How are these needs reflected socially, economically, ethnically, environmentally, politically and religiously?
- What area of our community is the furthest away from the vision that God would hold for our community?
- What special opportunities of connection and ministry are there within our sphere of influence (within a half mile)?
- What burning issues are alive in the public's eye and focused on in the media?
- What are the most significant changes in our community in the last decade, and what needs do these create?
- What are the largest community events, and what needs or opportunities do they create?
- Because of our unique location, what solution to community needs could we provide that no other church does?
- How would we describe the "atmosphere of lostness" in our community?
- How did our community come into existence? Does any of this suggest a role for us?
- Does the history of our community bring to light any spiritual strongholds?
- What one positive change in our community would have the most dramatic effect in people's lives?
- Who are the people we have been able to draw into the life of our congregation?
- How has our past prepared us for such a time as this?

GIFTING involves the unique resources and abilities that God has brought together in your church. God has not only placed you as a leader and your congregation in a specific place and time, He has provided your congregation with resources and abilities for you to be able to accomplish His mission and move toward His vision. The resources are collective and multifaceted: collective spiritual gifts, training and education, collective experiences, financial capabilities, creative capacities, shared possessions and a particular anointing of the Holy Spirit. Here are some questions that can help you and your leadership team explore your congregation's unique gifting.

- If a guest to your church was asked the question, "What did you like best about our church?" what would the guest say?
- If we were to stop nonmembers who drive by the church regularly and ask them how they feel about our church, what would they say?
- If our church suddenly was uprooted from the community, what would people in the community say they missed the most?
- How would a group of pastors or a denominational fellowship describe the strength of our church?
- What is the biggest impact our church has made in the community?
- What is the most significant thing our church could do in our community or in the world?
- Who comes to our church? How do ethnicity, age, gender, life stage, life issues and spiritual maturity define our congregation's make-up?
- What spiritual gifts seem to be most prominent in our church?
- What capabilities tend to cluster in our church?
- If we could only do one ministry outside our church walls, which would we choose?
- What atmosphere do we tend to create when our people get together?
- What need in the world in which we live would we most want to address?
- What do members say when they talk about what attracted them to the church?

PASSION involves what energizes and animates your leadership and your church. By passion I mean the sense of vitality and energy a congregation might possess. This passion is more than just your passion. The passion is the life-giving, energizing presence of the Holy Spirit in the community. To help you, here are some questions to reflect upon.

- What one thing bothers you most about the world?
- If you could not fail, what one thing would you pursue for God?
- What do you tend to pray for the most?
- What do you love doing most in your community or church?
- What gives you energy?
- What have you secretly believed you would be really good at if only you were given a chance?
- Who are your heroes? Why do you admire them?
- What would you want people saying about you at your funeral? What would they say you were and what would they say you accomplished?
- If there was one thing our church could accomplish, what would you want it to be?

Where the three circles of context, gifting and passion intersect is the focal point or sweet spot of your church's unique vision. The intersection of the three circles represent aspects of your church's God-given uniqueness and a focal point for considering God's unique vision for your church.

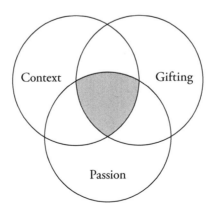

The focal point or sweet spot provides a kind of *"bullseye"* for your vision. Given your sweet spot, can you begin to imagine a possible future destination? What would it look like if you and your congregation were to move toward it?

EXERCISE: *Your church's sweet spot!*

The process of discerning your church's sweet spot requires a team and time to get a full picture. Gather your leadership team together and facilitate a brainstorming session to come up with answers to the questions: What do you see as your church's sweet spot? Given your sweet spot, can you begin to imagine a possible future destination? What would it look like if you and your congregation were to move toward it?

If your leadership team is not readily available, take some time personally to reflect on your church's context, gifting and passion and see if you could identify a few pieces of your church's sweet spot.

———————————————————————————————

———————————————————————————————

———————————————————————————————

———————————————————————————————

———————————————————————————————

———————————————————————————————

———————————————————————————————

EXPOSURE: *What is a vision frame?*

Do you remember the last time you sat down to do a jigsaw puzzle? The work proceeds in three basic steps. First, you take the pieces out of the box and turn them right-side up. The second part of the process is finding all the little pieces with straight edges to piece together the top and bottom and sides to form a frame. The process of putting a puzzle together is made easier by putting the border pieces together to form a frame. The third step is putting all the other pieces together to arrive at a complete picture.

Likewise, it is helpful in clarifying God's vision to begin with what is called a *"vision frame"* before trying to articulate your vision. The concept of *"vision frame"* comes from Will Mancini's, *Church Unique.* The vision frame consists of four pieces:

The first piece is **MISSION**. Mission answers the question: ***WHAT? What are we doing?***

Jesus articulated the mission of the church in what is referred to as *"the Great Commission."* Usually, when people think of the Great Commission, they think of Jesus' words in Matthew 28:18-20. But, in fact, Jesus spoke the Great Commission in all four Gospels, as well as, in the book of Acts. You will discover in looking at these five statements of Jesus' mission, that Jesus articulated the mission of the church in five different ways, using different language, suggesting that there is no one way to communicate the single mission of the church.

EXERCISE: The Great Commission

Take some time to read the Great Commission as it is found in Matthew 28:18-20, Mark 16:15, Luke 9:51-55, John 20:19-22 and Acts 1:9.

Gather your leadership team together and facilitate a brainstorming session to come up with answers to write a synopsis of the Great Commission that Christ gave His church.

_____

_____

_____

_____

_____

_____

_____

EXERCISE: Mission Statement

Gather your leadership team together and facilitate a brainstorming session to come up with answers to create a draft mission statement that is unique to your church and its context in fifteen words or less.

> **EXAMPLE**: *Our mission is to connect real people to Jesus through real relationships.*

> **EXAMPLE**: *We exist to lead people into a life-changing, ever-growing relationship with Jesus Christ.*

_____

_____

_____

_____

_____

_____

Will Mancini writes: *"The value of the Vision Frame is directly related to how well your words are crafted. When collaborating as a team on the Vision Frame, you will want to keep some rules for good articulation in mind. In my work with church leaders, I insist that they adhere to the 'five Cs' as our measure of success. The Vision Frame components must be clear, concise, compelling, catalytic, and contextual."* (Will Mancini, *Church Unique*, p. 116)

Ask these five questions of your mission statement draft:

- Is it **CLEAR?**—The first criteria is clarity. The first question that must be asked is this: Is our language clear enough that a twelve-year-old boy who has not been to church would understand?
- Is it **CONCISE?**—Any part of the Vision Frame should not be long, but short enough so that people will find it memorable and memorize-able. Attempt to describe God's vision for your congregation or organization in one breath.
- Is it **COMPELLING?**—Does the statement resonate with people so that they really like what it says, and they want to be a part of it?
- Is it **CATALYTIC?**—The *Vision Frame* statement should connect to the heart. The *Vision Frame* statements, as well as, the vision itself should inspire the listener to act. Choose words that create an emotional connection. Does the statement cause me to do something?
- Is it **CONTEXTUAL?**—Do the words communicate Biblical truths for the listener's time and place?

The second piece of the vision frame is **STRATEGY**. Strategy answers the question: *HOW? How are we carrying out the mission?* Strategy explains the specific pieces for how we carry out the mission, which provides a clear plan that people can join to participate in the mission.

EXAMPLE:

- ❖ Connect through life groups
- ❖ Commit through worship
- ❖ Contribute through gift-driven ministry
  (The Three Cs of the First Baptist Church, Everett, WA)

EXAMPLE:

Bless → Become → Belong →Bring → Build
(Calvary Baptist, Clearwater, FL)

EXERCISE: Gather your leadership team together and facilitate a brainstorming session to come up with the three or four key ministries your church engages in to accomplish the mission?

- _____
- _____
- _____
- _____

The third piece of the vision frame is **VALUES**. Values answer the question *WHY? Why are we doing it?* Think of values as the fuel for your organization or the passion, the emotion that propels your church to do what it does. More will be said about this important topic of values in Chapter 11, *The Value of Values.*

EXAMPLE:

- ❖ Relevant Truth
- ❖ Encompassing Grace
- ❖ Authentic Relationships
- ❖ Lifelong Serving

EXERCISE: Gather your leadership team together and facilitate a brainstorming session to come up with the 4 or 5 most important values that fuel why your church does what it does.

- ❖ _____
- ❖ _____
- ❖ _____
- ❖ _____

MARKS are the fourth piece of the vision frame. Marks answer the question **WHEN?** ***When are we successful?*** Marks represent points of progress towards the vision. Unfortunately, few churches or Christians have a clear and measurable definition of spiritual success.

Marks are sometimes referred to as Measures, Milestones, Goals, or Objectives. The value of a term like "Marks" is that when congregations use terms like *"goals, objectives, or measurements,"* they usually think restrictively in terms of attendance numbers and offering received. Marks, on the other hand, can be written to describe accomplishments of the congregation's progress toward the vision.

EXAMPLE:

> ❖ Five members trained to lead a life group by year end
> ❖ Three new life groups meeting by year end
> ❖ 30 percent of our life groups doing an outreach project by year end

Marks can also be written to describe the set of attributes or qualities in an individual's life that reflect the accomplishment of the church's mission. *"The Marks are the church's portrait of a disciple and definition of spiritual maturity."* (Will Mancini, *Church Unique*, p. 152) While setting an attendance goal or a financial goal can be quite simple, what is more challenging, yet most effective when it comes to vision are some quality marks that answer the questions, *"What qualities do we imagine seeing in the person who fully embraces the mission, strategy, and values of our church?"* This following example presents the Marks in the form of questions that members can ask themselves to assess if they are making progress toward the vision.

EXAMPLE:

> ❖ Do I meet daily with God?
> ❖ Am I growing in my relationships with those I am meeting weekly with in my small group?

❖ Am I intentionally building a relationship with someone far from God?
❖ Am I generous?
❖ Do I serve weekly using my spiritual gifts?

List what Marks or qualities of a follower of Jesus Christ you would hope for in your congregation. Complete the sentence, *"A follower of Jesus Christ will . .*

_____

_____

_____

_____

_____

_____

_____

The **VISION** itself is the picture within the vision frame, a picture of where God is leading. Vision answers the question **WHERE?** *Where is God taking us?*

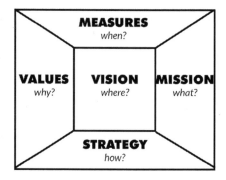

Imagine for a moment that you are going on vacation to Yellowstone National Park. You have talked with others about their trips to Yellowstone. You have researched and have beautiful colored brochures of the park. Think of the Yellowstone National Park brochures with the colorful pictures as the vision for your vacation, the destination.

Think of your vision statement as a full-color travel brochure. Looking at the brochure pictures create excitement and anticipation for the trip.

People ask, *"What is the difference between a vision statement and a mission statement?"* If the vision statement is our full-color travel brochure, the mission statement would be our compass providing direction and confirming that indeed we are heading in the right direction. Think of your mission statement as your compass and your vision statement as a full-color travel brochure.

Which do you think generates the most excitement, the compass or the brochure? The brochure, right? When you see the picture of the majestic mountains, the vast, expansive land and the animals roaming the countryside, your excitement and anticipation for the destination grows, doesn't it? This is the value of a compelling vision.

The brochure, however, does not tell you how to get there. What is needed is a map. Think of a map as the strategy, the directions. If the vision can be defined as our destination, then the vision path or strategy is our map. The strategy describes how we will get to our destination.

If the trip to Yellowstone National Park is several days, you will want to have stop-off points where you'll stop for the night before heading off the next morning, or places where you will stop for lunch or dinner. Think of these stop-off points as the marks or milestones along your journey. Along the vision path there will be milestones. "A milestone represents a point of progress that will be definitely reached or not." (Will Mancini, *Church Unique*, p. 189)

Are you beginning to see how all the pieces of the vision frame fit together? The vision frame provides a clear Biblical frame for the vision. The vision is a mental image of a preferred future. Establishing a focal point or sweet spot and a vision frame makes it easier to extrapolate a future picture for your church. What would it look like if you and your congregation began fulfilling your mission, fueled by your values, using your strategy and making progress toward God's vision for your congregation?

Receiving God's vision is both a visual and spiritual exercise. Because it is a visual exercise, the leader will want to have creative people working on the vision team. Imagination and possibility thinking should be encouraged.

Because it is a spiritual exercise, all the steps of this process must be approached prayerfully. If we are truly seeking God's vision, then we should be asking every step of the way, *"God, what is the vision you want us to see and pursue?"* So, before you go any further, take some time to pray and ask God to reveal His vision for you and those you are leading.

EXERCISE: Read the vision of Martin Luther King, Jr. found earlier in this chapter and describe the picture you see.

_____

_____

_____

_____

_____

_____

_____

EXERCISE: I have a dream!

Visualize what the future of your church or your organization would be like and the impact your organization would have if everything went exactly according to your dream. Moishe Rosen teaches a one sentence mental exercise that's an effective tool in creative dreaming. It is simply to finish this sentence: ***If I had*** _____

_____

_____

_____

_____

_____

I would _____

_____

_____

_____

_____

_____

EXPERIENCE: *Sharing your vision*

Share with your leadership team or with a group of other leaders what you wrote in the *"I have a dream…"* exercise above. If others completed this assignment, have each person share. After each person shares, have the group pray for the person, that God would make His vision clearer. Pray that the person would be open to any direction or redirection that God would want to give. Pray that the person would grow in their leadership to bring glory to God.

CHAPTER 4

THE CALLING OF
A LEADER

Exodus 3:11-4:17

KEY PRINCIPLE: RESPONDING TO GOD'S CALL REQUIRES FAITH.

"Without faith it is impossible to please God."
—Hebrews 11:6

EXPOSURE: God's vision is always God-size!

Leadership requires faith! Every leader will face challenges that tend to create fear, challenges that require a leader to exercise faith and courage if the leader hopes to be successful. Whether it be the fear of failure, the fear of inadequacy, the fear of making mistakes or the fear of criticism—to name just a few—to be a successful leader in any endeavor, you must have courageous faith!

Faith is especially needed in spiritual leadership because God's assignments are always ***GOD-SIZE***, which is to say beyond our human capacity. The things God will call upon us to do will require an incredible dependence upon God and faith to obey what God has called us to do. You should get comfortable with the fact that God's assignments are always ***GOD-SIZE!*** They normally elicit the response, *"Oh my! This is huge!"*

God's call on Moses' life and the particular assignment God had for Moses was **GOD-SIZE**. In the last chapter we saw how God called Moses to lead the people of Israel out of bondage in Egypt and gave Moses a vision of where he was to lead them, the Promise Land—*"a good and spacious land, a land flowing with milk and honey."*

God's vision for Moses was the possession of a promised land, while Moses and the people of Israel were still slaves in Egypt, in the firm grip of Pharaoh. God called Moses to lead approximately 2.5 million Israelites out of Egypt. *WOW!* This was a **GOD-SIZE** assignment!

Moses' assignment was **GOD-SIZE**. But God's assignments are always **GOD-SIZE**. Consider just a few of the assignments God has given to his chosen leaders in the Bible:

- God's vision for Noah was for Noah to lead in building a large ark for a coming flood when not one drop of rain had fallen. This was a **GOD-SIZE** assignment!
- God's vision for Joseph, when he was still a youth, was that he would grow up to become a great ruler. This was a **GOD-SIZE** assignment!
- God's vision for Joshua was that he would bring down the fortified walls of his enemies in Jericho by walking around the walls and blowing trumpets. This was a **GOD-SIZE** assignment!
- God's vision for the first century church, when it was only 120 strong, was that the church would make disciples not only in Jerusalem, but Judea, and Samaria, and even to all the world. This was a **GOD-SIZE** assignment!

Henry Blackaby says:

> *"Some people say, 'God will never ask me to do something I can't do.' I have come to a place in my life that, if the assignment I sense God is giving me is something that I know I can handle, I know it*

is probably not from God. The kind of assignments God gives in the Bible are always God-sized. They are always beyond what people can do, because he wants to demonstrate his nature, his strength, his provision, and his kindness to his people and to a watching world. That is the only way the world will come to know him."

Mark it down! God's assignments are always **GOD-SIZE**, and because they are, they usually cause us to wonder how we can possibly accomplish them! There will be a strong sense that the vision God has given us is impossible. And the truth is, without God, it is impossible!

EXERCISE: God-size assignments require faith in God!

Take a moment to assess your faith. What is your faith like? (Check all that apply)

- ☐ Sporadic
- ☐ Growing
- ☐ Shrinking
- ☐ Simple
- ☐ Small
- ☐ Consistent
- ☐ Complex
- ☐ Strong
- ☐ Obedient
- ☐ Inconsistent
- ☐ Wavering
- ☐ Other _____

EXPOSURE: Moses' response to God's vision

God's vision for Moses was certainly a *"GOD-SIZE"* vision. It's why Moses exclaimed, *"Who am I, that I should go to Pharaoh and bring the Israelites out of Egypt?"* (Exodus 3:11) Moses' self-doubt was evident from the beginning. As we look at Moses' initial response to God's vision, we are going to hear some familiar excuses for why all of us tend to shrink back from God's vision for our lives.

Read about Moses' response to God's vision in Exodus 3:11-22.

[11] But Moses said to God, "Who am I, that I should go to Pharaoh and bring the Israelites out of Egypt?" [12] And God said, "I will be with you. And this will be the sign to you that it is I who have sent you: When you have brought the people out of Egypt, you will worship God on this mountain." [13] Moses said to God, "Suppose I go to the Israelites and say to them, 'The God of your fathers has sent me to you,' and they ask me, 'What is his name?' Then what shall I tell them?" [14] God said to Moses, "I AM WHO I AM. This is what you are to say to the Israelites: 'I AM has sent me to you.'" [15] God also said to Moses, "Say to the Israelites, 'The LORD, the God of your fathers—the God of Abraham, the God of Isaac and the God of Jacob—has sent me to you.' This is my name forever, the name by which I am to be remembered from generation to generation. [16] "Go, assemble the elders of Israel and say to them, 'The LORD, the God of your fathers—the God of Abraham, Isaac and Jacob—appeared to me and said: I have watched over you and have seen what has been done to you in Egypt. [17] And I have promised to bring you up out of your misery in Egypt into the land of the Canaanites, Hittites, Amorites, Perizzites, Hivites and Jebusites—a land flowing with milk and honey.' [18] "The elders of Israel will listen to you. Then you and the elders are to go to the king of Egypt and say to him, 'The LORD, the God of the Hebrews, has met with us. Let us take a three-day journey into the desert to offer sacrifices to the LORD our God.' [19] But I know that the king of Egypt will not let you go unless a mighty hand compels him. [20] So I will stretch out my hand and strike the Egyptians with all the wonders that I will perform among them. After that, he will let you go. [21] "And I will make the Egyptians favorably disposed toward this people, so that when you leave you will not go empty-handed. [22] Every woman is to ask her neighbor and any woman living in her house for articles of silver and gold and for clothing, which you will put on your sons and daughters. And so, you will plunder the Egyptians."

Let's look at Moses' responses to God's call, Moses' four objections to him being the right person for the assignment:

OBJECTION #1: *"Moses said to God, 'Who am I, that I should go to Pharaoh and bring the Israelites out of Egypt?'"* (Exodus 3:11) Moses felt that he couldn't possibly do what God called him to do. He felt like a *nobody.* Moses' problem was that he was more focused on himself than he was on the One who had called him and had given him a vision. That's often our problem too. Our focus is more on ourselves than it is on our great God.

Sometimes as Christians, and especially as leaders, we know what God has called us to do, but something always gets in the way of us feeling confident in these God-sized assignments. There resides within us a deep-seated belief that *"We're not capable."* We become overwhelmed by feelings of insecurity.

Ernesto decided to attend a leadership training event as he is very passionate about leading others. When he arrived however, he noticed that there were other leaders at the training event who were much more experienced than he was. He began to feel insecure and he hesitated to participate. When the speaker asked for participants to help during the training, he wouldn't raise his hand to volunteer because he began comparing himself to all the other leaders.

These feelings of inferiority can keep us from becoming the leader God designed and the leader God desires us to be. The word "inferior" comes from the word that means *"low"* or *"below."* People who have experienced disrespect or significant criticism by authority figures—anyone in a position *"above"* them—whether it is their parents, a supervisor at a job, or someone older, will experience deep-seated feelings of inferiority.

We have all had experiences where we felt as though we weren't good enough to accomplish something. We think anyone else would be more capable than us.

Why would feelings of inferiority be a topic of leadership? Well, our self-image colors and shapes our perception of what we can or cannot accomplish. If we see ourselves as inferior to others, then this inferior self-image will guarantee our lack of confidence to do anything significant. We might shrink back from any assignment that God might have for us. If, on the other hand, we are aware of our emotions and our feelings of inferiority, we can choose to exercise faith rather than allow our fear to determine what we will attempt to do for God.

EXERCISE: *Processing our feelings of inferiority*

Think of a time when the power and frequency of criticism (whether verbal or non-verbal), made you feel inferior. If possible, select a time related to your current feelings of inferiority. Write a description of that time.

_____

_____

_____

_____

_____

_____

_____

_____

Once you have written down one of several memories above, ask yourself these questions:

- What were you thinking when the person made you feel inferior?
- What emotions did you experience and how did your self-talk change?
- How long did these feelings and thoughts last?

- Have you been able to share these feelings of inferiority with anyone? If not, is there someone with whom you can share your real self and receive grace?

The powerful lesson we can learn from identifying and processing our feelings of inferiority is that people's criticism and negative feedback can begin to have less power over us when we learn that it isn't the event that make us inferior; it is our chosen reaction to the event that create feelings of inferiority. It is the thoughts and feelings we experience in response to the event that determine whether we choose feelings of inferiority or choose to exercise faith.

As leaders, it is important to discern where feelings of inferiority come from in order to grow in your faith. We need to process our feelings. If not, you could possibly say *"no"* to assignments God has for you by giving into feelings of inferiority, just like Moses almost did.

Feelings of inferiority in the leader can be a major roadblock to God accomplishing all that He wants to accomplish through you. It can be extremely helpful in dealing with inferiority feelings to sit down and share your struggle with these feelings with a mentor, or friend or counselor. Sharing with someone else, who could help you process your thoughts and feelings, could be an opportunity for you to overcome and be set free from these self-limiting feelings to become the leader God designed you to be.

Notice God's reply to Moses' objection. God's response to Moses was, *"I will be with you."* (Exodus 3:12) What God offered Moses is his **PRESENCE**. Vision, when it is God's vision, is always accompanied by God's presence. So, remember: When God calls you to do something great, when God gives you a great vision, He promises to accompany you as you take the steps to implement the vision.

Yes! God offers us his **PRESENCE**. He says that He is here with us. But we must do our part and be faithful in doing what He asks, regardless of what we feel.

"Yes! God offers his presence to remind us how He sees us. His presence emboldens us, motivates us to BE who He sees we are, and DO what He has called us to do.

Take a moment to reflect on how Moses saw himself. How do you imagine God saw Moses given his God-given assignment? How do you think this relates to you? How does this speak to you personally?"

OBJECTION #2: *"Moses said to God, 'Suppose I go to the Israelites and say to them, 'The God of your fathers has sent me to you,' and they ask me, 'What is his name?' Then what shall I tell them?'"* (Exodus3:13)

Moses was saying, *"I am not an authority!"* Have you ever felt that way, felt that you were no authority? I think a lot of us fear that God will call us to do something for which we will not know the correct answer, or we won't know the right thing to do.

Adela grew up feeling very strongly that she was a leader and had a lot to contribute, especially when it came to speaking with conviction around social justice issues. However, Adela was plagued with daily thoughts of self-doubt that created feelings of fear. Her thoughts included: *Will people listen to me as I am often younger and less experienced than some of the people I am speaking with? What if they discount me because I am a woman? What if at some point they find out that I don't know the answers to their questions or the right thing to do? What if people think I am too pushy in sharing my convictions?*

Fear is not always bad. For instance, if we are facing real danger, fear is a warning. Fear signals perceived danger and allows us time to defend ourselves or confront the threat or flee from the threat (fight or flight response). Where the challenge comes is discerning whether the perceived danger is real or imaginary.

One of the fears that confronts Christians, and particularly Christian leaders, is the fear generated by self-doubt. When God invited Moses to approach Pharaoh, he felt threatened and self-doubt gripped him. Moses' fear of Pharaoh generated self-doubt in Moses.

Fear is a tool that our enemy, Satan, frequently uses to keep us from doing what God has called us to do. Let us not forget that there is a spiritual battle going on, and Satan would like nothing more than to keep us fear filled.

The truth is that at the root of fear to do what God has called us to do is a lack of trust in God. Countless places in the Bible we are told to *"fear not"* but to *"trust in the Lord."* To trust in the Lord is a choice. However, if we are not aware of our fear, we cannot make this choice away from fear to trust in the Lord.

God's answer to our self-doubt as a spiritual leader is providing His authority. *"God said to Moses, "I AM WHO I AM. This is what you are to say to the Israelites: 'I AM has sent me to you.' God also said to Moses, 'Say to the Israelites, 'The LORD, the God of your fathers—the God of Abraham, the God of Isaac and the God of Jacob—has sent me to you. This is my name forever, the name you shall call me from generation to generation.'"* (Exodus 3:14-15)

In response to Moses' reluctance, God revealed to Moses his personal name. God told Moses, *"You just tell them that I AM WHO I AM sent you."* God's name is I AM WHO I AM, or I WILL BE WHO I WILL BE. In disclosing to Moses His personal name, God was saying to Moses, you have all the authority you need; you have my **PERMISSION**.

This was to be the source of Moses' authority as a leader. All spiritual leaders derive their authority from their relationship with God, and people's perception of that intimate relationship. God disclosed His name and then, adds *"the God of Abraham, the God of Isaac and the God of Jacob"* to help Moses see that he is linked to the leadership of past great leaders, and Moses could draw authority from walking in their footsteps.

What God offers us for any assignment He gives us is His **PERMISSION**. When we begin to feel the least bit of self-doubt, we need to keep in mind God's word to Moses, *"I AM has sent me to you."* As spiritual leaders, we carry out our assignment under the authority of God with His permission!

Then God said to Moses: *"Go, assemble the elders of Israel and say to them, 'The* LORD, *the God of your fathers—the God of Abraham, Isaac and Jacob—appeared to me and said: I have watched over you and have seen what has been done to you in Egypt."* (Exodus 3:16) God sent Moses to gather the elders and share with them that God had authorized him to lead the people out of Egypt.

I think God pressed Moses for this connection with the elders in order to win the people's confidence and support. Leaders must be *strategic* in bringing other leaders and influencers into the leadership process. Even though leaders are granted authority, they must still gain the support and participation of at least some of those who hold power already. What God was doing was creating a leadership team.

EXERCISE: Processing our fears

Explore the questions below regarding your own fears:

- What fears do you have about becoming the leader God wants you to be?
- What specific ways are you going to challenge your distortions and fears?
- How do you imagine God's words, *"I AM has sent me to you"* impacting your courage and faith in carrying out a God-given assignment?

OBJECTION #3: *"Moses answered, 'What if they do not believe me or listen to me and say, 'The LORD did not appear to you'?"* (Exodus 4:1)

Moses was concerned that the Israelites would neither listen to him nor follow his leadership. He was convinced that Pharaoh, will not take him seriously or believe what he had to say. He felt like an imposter.

God tried to reassure Moses that He would accomplish powerful things through him by responding to Moses' objection with a question: *"What is that in your hand?"* Moses replied, *"A staff."* The Lord said, *"Throw it on the ground."*

Moses threw it on the ground, and it became a snake, and he ran from it. Then the Lord said to him, "Reach out your hand and take it by the tail." So, Moses reached out and took hold of the snake and it turned back into a staff in his hand. "This," said the Lord, "is so that they may believe that the Lord, the God of their fathers—the God of Abraham, the God of Isaac and the God of Jacob—has appeared to you." (Exodus 4:2-5)

The rod was a symbol which, according to the rabbinic tradition, had been in the possession of the leader of every generation going back to Adam in the Garden of Eden. It was a symbol of authority, of power. Like all leaders, Moses possessed the rod and all he had to do was to believe that he had the power, the ability, to lead. All he had to do was act.

What God was demonstrating and offering to Moses was his **POWER**. God attempted to reassure Moses by demonstrating God's power at his disposal. Every leader should be reassured by this truth: God's calling and vision, are not only accompanied by God's presence and permission, but it is also accompanied by God's **POWER**! Moses' problem was that he was too focused on his own inability rather than the supernatural ability of the One who had called him and who gave him a vision. God was reminding Moses that he had God's power.

It is common for leaders to feel intimidated by people. Our excessive need to have peoples' approval and reassurance to make a decision or take action is another fear that every leader must address to be an effective leader. This need is really rooted in a fear of people's disapproval which can paralyze us from doing what God has clearly called us to do. Even worse, this excessive need for people's approval and need for people's reassurance, and fear of their disapproval, can drive us to live a life of trying to please people rather than pleasing God.

The feeling that *"I must do whatever everyone wants of me"* can be a serious detriment to doing what God has called us to do. If we chose to do something based on what others will think, we'll fail to do what God has called us to do. Jesus warned about excessive people pleasing when He said, *"Woe to you when all men speak well of you, for that is how their fathers treated the false prophets."* (Luke 6:26)

The Apostle Paul, who was a key leader in the first century missionary movement of the church, reflected on his own leadership with respect to pleasing people, writing: *"Am I now trying to win the approval of men, or of God? Or am I trying to please men? If I were still trying to please men, I would not be a servant of Christ."* (Galatians 1:10)

It is essential that leaders not fear people nor make decisions based on fear. Jesus did not fear people. He loved people. He spoke truth with grace. Instead of worrying about what individuals would think, Jesus simply exercised His leadership and left it with people whether they liked what He did or said, or not. Jesus was not driven by a need to have everyone like Him or follow Him.

The Gospel writer, John, testified about Jesus: *"23 Now while he was in Jerusalem at the Passover Festival, many people saw the signs he was performing and believed in his name. 24 But Jesus would not entrust himself to them, for he knew all people. 25 He did not need any testimony about mankind, for he knew what was in each person."* (John 2:23-25)

To avoid this people-pleasing tendency, the spiritual leader needs to be deeply rooted in God's love. People, who have been unable to risk showing their real self to others, may still think they are unlovable.

They don't realize that our *"lovability"* rests, not on our own merit, but on the ability of the one doing the loving. Approval can be earned, but love can't.

The power of God's love can help a leader experience God's unconditional acceptance and approval. Then, and only then, can the leader lead out of a healthy place of having already been accepted and approved by the important One, so that there is not this excessive need for approval by everyone.

EXERCISE: Processing our people-pleasing tendency

Answer the questions below regarding your own fears:

- On a scale between 0-10 rate your need for peoples' approval. ____
- Why do you think you had the score you did?

  _____

  _____

- In what ways does God's unconditional love for you empower you to lead?

  _____

  _____

OBJECTION #4: *"Moses said to the Lord, "Pardon your servant, Lord. I have never been eloquent, neither in the past nor since you have spoken to your servant. I am slow of speech and tongue."* (Exodus 4:10) This objection, by Moses, for not stepping up to God's call on our life is a common one: *"I am not a great communicator!"*

Nestor was feeling prompted by God to start a new ministry, but he felt as though he might be discovered as an inadequate leader or might be lacking in some way if he took the lead. He felt as though he didn't fit the mold of a *"leader"* as most people define a leader. While Nestor was a good communicator and an exceptional motivator, he was not very organized. To everyone else, Nestor seemed confident, but when Nestor was honest with himself, he thought: *"What is the sense of trying? I'll never be able to organize this. I mean, I've tried in the past, but I am just not good with details."*

Those of us who have experienced failure can seriously question our own personal competence in the present. Perhaps we've tried something in the past, and because we were given little direction or guidance, we weren't successful. Perhaps we never received enough positive reinforcement or clear feedback from others about our talents and abilities, leaving us unclear about our strengths so that we ended up focusing on our weaknesses and failures.

An important aspect of our identity is our talents and abilities that God gives us. God gives each of us talents/abilities and holds us responsible for using them and developing them. Unfortunately, many of us are unclear about our strengths. When we aren't clear about our strengths, often we'll tend to focus on our inadequacies and deficiencies.

Focusing on our inadequacies and deficiencies will have a very negative effect on us as leaders. Leaders who feel inadequate may have difficulties in establishing healthy, long-lasting relationships, scaring others away by our defensive attitudes. As in the case of Moses, we may say *"no"* to God's calling because of feeling *"not capable enough."*

However, what we are seeing in this story is that for every objection Moses raised, God had an answer. *"[11] The Lord said to him, "Who gave human beings their mouths? Who makes them deaf or mute? Who gives them sight or makes them blind? Is it not I, the Lord? [12] Now go; I will help you speak and will teach you what to say."* (Exodus 4:11-12) God offered Moses his **PROVISION**.

If we imagine that the responsibility for success rests with us, if we are egotistical enough to think that it all depends on us, then like Moses we will feel grossly inadequate. God reminded Moses, and us, that He is the

Creator of mouths and speech. God is the Creator of ears to hear. God promised to help Moses speak and to teach Moses exactly what to say.

Yet, despite all of God's reassurances, Moses pleaded, *"Please, O Lord, send someone else!"* It could not have been clearer. Moss honestly believed that anyone would be a better candidate to complete the mission than him.

How ironic! Moses, who was destined to become one of the most renowned lawgivers and poets in human history, felt at the outset that he lacked the ability to articulate God's vision, a vision the people would come to embrace if they could trust his leadership.

God responded one more time. *"14 Then the Lord's anger burned against Moses and he said, "What about your brother, Aaron the Levite? I know he can speak well. He is already on his way to meet you, and he will be glad to see you. 15 You shall speak to him and put words in his mouth; I will help both of you speak and will teach you what to do. 16 He will speak to the people for you, and it will be as if he were your mouth and as if you were God to him."* (Exodus 4:14-16) Again God offers PROVISION in the form of Moses' brother, Aaron.

Moses' problem was that he was too focused on his inabilities rather than the abilities God had provided him and abilities God would provide through others like Aaron. As leaders we need to understand that God has gifted us with abilities. We have strengths. Yes, we also have weaknesses and deficiencies. But we can trust that *where God guides, God will provide.* If we respond positively to God's call in faith, if we take up the vision God gives us, then we can be assured of God's **PROVISION**.

EXERCISE: *Processing the fear of our inability*

- What negative experience in life have caused you to conclude *"I can't"*?

  _____

  _____

  _____

  _____

  _____

- What did you learn about yourself from those two negative experiences?

  _____

  _____

  _____

  _____

- What are your strengths, abilities or gifting that make you the person God created you to be? Do others know this about you?

  _____

  _____

  _____

  _____

EXPERIENCE: *Receiving the Vision*

Reflect on Moses' four objections to being qualified to take God's vision to the people and Pharaoh. Which one is more likely to be used by you when you learn of God's *"GOD-SIZE"* vision for you? If not one of Moses' objections, what objection can you imagine speaking when you learn of God's *"**GOD-SIZE**"* vision for you? Write out your answer and, in a group of three or four, share this truth about yourself.

_____

_____

_____

_____

_____

_____

In this chapter, we've looked at Moses' four objections or excuses for why he didn't feel qualified to lead the people of Israel toward God's vision of *"a good and spacious land, a land flowing with milk and honey."* Every leader, when approaching a **GOD-SIZE** vision, will question their qualifications at some point. Keep in mind the principle shared in chapter one: *"God doesn't call the qualified, He qualifies the called."*

Take some time to reflect on what God promised Moses as a leader. God promises the same to you! If you believe that God has called you to lead, what are God's promises to you that should bolster your courage? Write out your response and, in groups of three or four, share your confidence and courage in the Lord.

_____

_____

_____

_____

_____

_____

CHAPTER 5

BETTER TOGETHER

Exodus 4:27-31

KEY PRINCIPLE: BRINGING ABOUT TRANSFORMATIONAL CHANGE REQUIRES A TEAM.

"Though one may be overpowered, two can defend themselves.
A cord of three strands is not quickly broken."
—Ecclesiastes 4:12

EXPOSURE: Getting People on Your Team

While God begins with a leader, significant transformational change is never accomplished alone. Our tendency is to look at any significant change or achievement and connect it to a highly visible leader, failing to realize that the accomplishment required the partnership of many persons.

For instance, consider the Civil Rights Movement in America, and we think of Martin Luther King, Jr. Mention the Missionaries of Charity in Calcutta, India and immediately Mother Teresa comes to mind. It is easy to conclude that great accomplishments or movements like these are brought about by the efforts of a single visionary leader and miss a critical component necessary for bringing about significant change and transformation. Transformational change requires a team!

Similarly, Moses is often seen as the one who led the people of Israel out of bondage in Egypt to the Promise Land. But if we conclude that Moses accomplished this arduous task alone, we will have made a serious mistake. Learn about Moses' vision team by reading Exodus 3:16-20.

> *"16 Go, assemble the elders of Israel and say to them, 'The Lord, the God of your fathers—the God of Abraham, Isaac and Jacob—appeared to me and said: I have watched over you and have seen what has been done to you in Egypt. 17 And I have promised to bring you up out of your misery in Egypt into the land of the Canaanites, Hittites, Amorites, Perizzites, Hivites and Jebusites—a land flowing with milk and honey.' 18 "The elders of Israel will listen to you. Then you and the elders are to go to the king of Egypt and say to him, 'The Lord, the God of the Hebrews, has met with us. Let us take a three-day journey into the desert to offer sacrifices to the Lord our God.' 19 But I know that the king of Egypt will not let you go unless a mighty hand compels him. 20 So I will stretch out my hand and strike the Egyptians with all the wonders that I will perform among them. After that, he will let you go . . . ."*

EXERCISE: Moses and the Elders

Why do you think God insisted that Moses gather the elders to share with them what God had spoken to Moses?

_____

_____

_____

_____

What do you imagine to be the wisdom of sharing about his conversation with God with the elders?

_____

_____

_____

_____

To whom did God give the assignment to talk to the king of Egypt?

_____

_____

_____

_____

Do you have a leadership team? If you do, name the members of your leadership team and the role they play on your team. If you do not have a leadership team, use this space below to reflect on and write why you think you do not have a team.

_____

_____

_____

_____

Do you share authority with your leadership team? Give an example of you sharing authority with another leader.

_____

_____

_____

_____

EXPOSURE: Moses and Aaron

In the prior chapter, we read how Moses felt that he was an inadequate communicator. Interestingly, Steven Hayward, in his book *Churchill on Leadership*, points out: *"Many modern-day leaders suffer from speech impediments and work hard to overcome them. Winston Churchill had a lisp, which he struggled to correct. And Churchill perhaps will best be remembered for his inspiring speeches during the battle for Britain. Part of what enabled him to become such a great communicator was how the British people responded to his leadership initiatives."* (Hayward, Churchill on Leadership, pp. 98-99) Even great leaders need the faith and support of people around them to overcome obstacles or shortcomings.

God provided Aaron to assist Moses in communicating the vision God had given to him and to serve on Moses' vision team. Leaders cannot succeed on their own. The most effective leaders choose to partner with capable individuals whose skills and knowledge compliment their own. Unfortunately, many leaders find it difficult to share ministry responsibility.

Aaron will be a key leader in the Israelites' journey to the Promise Land. But Aaron will play a kind of *"second fiddle"* to Moses, which is not an easy instrument to play. When asked what the most difficult instrument in the orchestra is, Leonard Bernstein once responded: *"The second fiddle. I can get plenty of first violinists, but to find someone who can play the second fiddle with enthusiasm – that's a problem; and if we have no second fiddle, we have no harmony."*

The most important choice a leader can make is designating his or her second in command. The number-two person is the most important hire and must be someone who balances the leader's strengths and temperament, shows loyalty without being a *"yes"* person, and has the ability for working well with a variety of individuals and groups.

God spoke directly to both Moses and Aaron, telling them what they should say to the Israelites and to Pharaoh. Aaron emerged as a full partner with Moses. His role was not limited to speaking to the Israelites just what Moses wanted said. Aaron, along with Moses, addressed the Israelites and Pharaoh. Moses didn't stand alone; Aaron shared the burden and the challenge with him.

In Exodus 4:29-31 we read: *"²⁹ Moses and Aaron brought together all the elders of the Israelites, ³⁰ and Aaron told them everything the Lord had said to Moses. He also performed the signs before the people, ³¹ and they believed.*

And when they heard that the Lord was concerned about them and had seen their misery, they bowed down and worshiped."

In taking this step, Moses and Aaron got the elders on board *their vision team*. What do I mean by *"vision team"*? A vision team is a diverse group of key members of your congregation or organization who join the leader in discerning, shaping and implementing God's vision for the congregation or the organization.

EXPOSURE: *The process of establishing a vision statement*

The process of establishing a vision statement is best accomplished with a team. A vision team should be involved early in the process of establishing a vision statement, as well as, helping lead the change process, and working in partnership with the leader until the end of the process. The process of establishing the vision frame and vision statement, gaining vision team consensus, and communicating the vision to gain greater support for the vision statement involves the following steps:

> Prayerfully seek God's vision through the vision frame process → Leader writes first draft of vision statement → Seek feedback from vision team → Revise/Second Draft → Obtain Feedback/Develop Consensus → Expand consensus group

EXPOSURE: *What does a vision team do?*

- **A vision team works with the leader through the vision frame process.**

- **Once the vision frame is established, the visionary leader writes a first draft of a vision statement. Most often a vision and vision statement are initiated by a single person, the leader. A leader**

brings the first draft of the vision statement to the vision team for the team's feedback.

Four critical questions to ask the vision team about the proposed vision statement:

1. What is your overall reaction to the vision statement?
2. What questions about the meaning of the vision do you have?
3. Are there concepts or ideas that should be added or omitted?
4. Are there better ways of saying it?

These are important questions for the leader to ask the vision team. The input from the vision team is essential in the shaping of the vision statement.

- **A vision team helps shape the vision.** As the vision team helps shape the vision statement, an important thing happens. The vision team begins to own the vision as its own. I generally counsel leaders to seek the vision team's input in order to get the vision team's fingerprints all over the vision statement. The greater the ownership, the greater will be the commitment of the team to partner with the leader in communicating the vision and assisting the change process.

- **A vision team confirms the vision as God's vision for the church or organization.** This is critical. If you, as the leader, cannot get consensus support from the vision team for the vision statement, you are unlikely to get support for it in the larger congregation or in the larger organization when you go public.

"If a deep and shared commitment cannot be achieved, true transformation is not possible." (Jim Herrington, Mike Bonem and James Furr, *Leading Congregational Change*, p. 54)

- **A vision team helps cast and communicate the vision.** The value of a diverse group of key members of your congregation or organization on the vision team is, that when it comes to communicating the vision to the larger congregation or larger organization, these members will have enormous influence; more influence than you would have as a leader by yourself.

- **A vision team helps create the critical mass necessary for beginning the process of change.** In order to bring about significant change and transformation, a significant core of the members of your congregation or your organization must ultimately embrace the vision and the change implied by the vision. People come from different backgrounds and experiences, and a diverse enough team contributes to making sure the vision is capturing as many aspects of the congregation as possible. By involving the vision team early in the change process and working with the team to embrace the vision, you will begin creating that critical mass essential for successful change and transformation to take place.

EXERCISE: Who would you select for your vision team?

Write down the names of two or three persons who immediately come to mind who you would trust to share your vision:

_____

_____

_____

_____

EXPOSURE: Who should serve on the vision team?

- **People who have power and influence in the congregation.** Vision team members do not have to be persons presently in formal leadership roles or positions. In fact, sometimes it is better that they are not. Persons outside the formal leadership structure can provide an important perspective.

- **People who adequately represent the constituencies in the congregation.** You will want to have broad and diverse representation of the various constituencies in your congregation or organization. This could include age, gender, experience, etc.

- **People who can make a meaningful contribution, each person willing to share his or her unique gifts.** Multiple gifts are needed on a vision team. Each member of the team should be willing to share what he or she can give best.

- **People who will be open to the process and who will work within the process.** The process requires a lot of give and take. Therefore, vision team members need to be spiritually mature, good listeners, and not contentious.

- **Appropriate staff and board representation. In most congregations or organizations there is a formal approval group.** That group should be represented so that the vision team does not commit a lot of effort to arrive at a vision statement only to discover that the formal approval group has serious concerns or reservations.

EXERCISE: Now that you have looked at some guidelines for selecting vision team members, who would you select to assist you in the work of creating a vision frame and vision statement? Give some further thought to who should be included on your vision team. Write the names of the persons you would invite to be on your team and in one sentence explain why you have chosen them.

_____

_____

_____

_____

_____

_____

EXPOSURE: *What makes a good team?*

- **A clear and common objective.** Without a clear and common objective, a vision team will flounder. In general, the objective of a vision team for a congregation or a religious organization is to prayerfully discern God's vision for the congregation or organization.

- **A high level of trust.** Without a high level of trust, members of a vision team will not feel safe to share their deepest aspirations and true feelings. Team is a highly relational entity and the foundation of all relationships is trust. A leader will want to address the importance of high-level trust and help the team establish any guidelines that will ensure a trust-based culture in the first meeting.

- **Open communication.** Without open communication, divergent opinions and perhaps the best ideas will not be shared.

EXPERIENCE: *Seeking feedback*

Break into groups of three or four. Each person should have ten minutes to share their draft vision statement and ask group members the following four questions:

1. What is your overall reaction to the vision statement I've drafted?
2. Do you have any questions about the meaning of the vision?
3. In your opinion, are there concepts or ideas that should be added or omitted?
4. Can you imagine a better way of saying it?

CHAPTER 6

RESISTANCE TO THE LEADER

Exodus 5-10

KEY PRINCIPLE: CHANGE AND TRANSFORMATION WILL BE MET BY RESISTANCE. THEREFORE, EXPECT RESISTANCE!

Question: *How many Baptists does it take to change a light bulb?*

EXPOSURE: Expect resistance!

Resistance to change is such a common experience in churches that we have the following:

How many **Charismatics** does it take to change a light bulb?
Answer: Only one since his/her hands are in the air anyway.

How many **Calvinists** does it take to change a light bulb?
Answer: None. God has predestined when the light will be on. Calvinists do not change light bulbs. They simply read the instructions and pray the light bulb will be one that has been chosen to be changed.

How many **TV evangelists** does it take to change a light bulb?
Answer: One. But for the message of light to continue, send in your donation today.

How many **independent fundamentalists** does it take to change a light bulb?

Answer: Only one, because any more might result in too much cooperation.

How many **Catholics** does it take to change a light bulb?

Answer: None. They always use candles.

How many **Pentecostals** does it take to change a light bulb?

Answer: One to change the bulb and nine to pray against the spirit of darkness.

How many **worship leaders** who use guitars does it take to change a light bulb?

Answer: One. But soon all those around can warm up to its glowing.

How many **Lutherans** does it take to change a light bulb?

Answer: One to change the bulb, and nine to say how much they liked the old one.

How many **United Methodists** does it take to change a light bulb?

Answer: This statement was issued— *"We choose not to make a statement either in favor of or against the need for a light bulb. However, if in your own journey you have found that a light bulb works for you, that is fine."*

How many **Amish** does it take to change a light bulb?

Answer: *"What's a light bulb?"*

How many **youth pastors** does it take to change a light bulb?

Answer: Youth pastors aren't around long enough for a light bulb to burn out.

How many **Presbyterians** does it take to change a light bulb?

Answer: There is some question here. But we have it on good authority that they have appointed a committee to study the issue and report back at their next meeting.

How many **Baptists** does it take to change a light bulb?

Answer: *"Change? You're not going to changes things, are you?"*

--Author unknown

Change is not just challenging for churches. Most people find change challenging. Resistance to change is a natural human reaction. As a leader, you should expect resistance when you introduce a new vision or new direction, and you should not be surprised when people begin resisting the change you are introducing.

Younger and inexperienced leaders typically underestimate the challenge of leading change. Many find themselves surprised that the majority of people have at least an initial negative reaction to change. Most surprising to younger and inexperienced leaders is that people will resist even positive change. Do not underestimate resistance you will receive when you begin disturbing people's *"comfort zone"* of the status quo.

EXERCISE: Assessing resistance in your own congregation or organization

Respond to the following statements by using the following scale:

1. Strongly disagree
2. Disagree
3. Neither agree nor disagree
4. Agree
5. Strongly agree

_____ My congregation's (or organization's) culture values conservative, cautious directions.

_____ Most of the changes we see are incremental in nature.

_____ We tend to avoid deep and bold changes.

_____ *There is a short-term, day-to-day approach to ministry with little long-term planning.*

_____ Persons in leadership focus on management (maintaining) more than leadership (change).

_____ People have little hope about the future of our congregation or organization.

_____ There are obvious changes needed, but no one seems willing to initiate.

_____ Discussion of failure to make needed changes is very rare. (Adapted from *How to Change Your Church-without killing it* by Alan Nelson & Gene Appel)

After responding to the statements above, what thoughts do you have about your congregation's or organization's resistance level?

_____

_____

_____

_____

_____

_____

_____

EXPOSURE: Moses faced resistance

In Exodus, chapters 5-10, we read the familiar story of Moses coming before Pharaoh and demanding that Pharaoh let God's people go. Moses did not come before Pharaoh once, but many times. Even after God communicated His seriousness about His demands by sending plagues, still Pharaoh refused to let God's people go. Take a few moments to review the pattern of Moses' demand of "letting God's people go" and Pharaoh's response.

First conversation

Moses demanded: "Let my people go." (Exodus 5:1)

Pharaoh responded: "Who is the LORD, that I should obey him and let Israel go? I do not know the LORD and I will not let Israel go." (Exodus (5:2) Pharaoh refused and then persecuted the Israelite slaves even more.

Exodus 5:6-14

⁶ That same day Pharaoh gave this order to the slave drivers and overseers in charge of the people: ⁷ "You are no longer to supply the people with straw for making bricks; let them go and gather their own straw. ⁸ But require them to make the same number of bricks as before; don't reduce the quota. They are lazy; that is why they are crying out, 'Let us go and sacrifice to our God.' ⁹ Make the work harder for the people so that they keep working and pay no attention to lies." ¹⁰ Then the slave drivers and the overseers went out and said to the people, "This is what Pharaoh says: 'I will not give you any more straw. ¹¹ Go and get your own straw wherever you can find it, but your work will not be reduced at all.'" ¹² So the people scattered all over Egypt to gather stubble to use for straw. ¹³ The slave drivers kept pressing them, saying, "Complete the work required of you for each day, just as when you had straw." ¹⁴ And Pharaoh's slave drivers beat the Israelite overseers they had appointed, demanding, "Why haven't you met your quota of bricks yesterday or today, as before?"

Is it any wonder that Moses' confidence in his mission and his desire to proceed were completely deflated following Pharaoh's refusal to let the Israelites leave? Moses lashed out at God: *"²²Why, Lord, why have you brought trouble on this people? Is this why you sent me? ²³ Ever since I went to Pharaoh to speak in your name, he has brought trouble on this people, and you have not rescued your people at all."* (Exodus 5:22-23)

One of the real tests of our leadership often comes down to this: How do we respond when things don't go the way we thought they would? How do we respond when we get a little *"push back"* or face resistance?

God reassured Moses, saying, *"¹ Now you will see what I will do to Pharaoh: Because of my mighty hand he will let them go; because of my mighty hand he will drive them out of his country." ² God also said to Moses, "I am the LORD. ³ I appeared to Abraham, to Isaac and to Jacob as God Almighty, but by my name the LORD did not make myself fully known to them. ⁴ I also established my covenant with them to give them the land of Canaan, where they resided as foreigners. ⁵ Moreover, I have heard the groaning of the Israelites, whom the Egyptians are enslaving, and I have remembered my covenant.⁶ "Therefore, say to the Israelites: 'I am the LORD, and I will bring you out from under the yoke of the Egyptians. I will free you from being slaves to them, and I will redeem you with an outstretched arm and with mighty acts of judgment."* (Exodus 6:1-6) God reassured Moses that it would be His power that guaranteed their deliverance.

"Moses reported this to the Israelites, but they did not listen to him because of their discouragement and harsh labor." (Exodus 6:9) Their reaction was totally understandable, wasn't it? Utterly demoralized because of their suffering, they gave up hope completely.

This is one the greatest challenges leaders have to confront: how to maintain hope in the face of their followers' inability to respond to their initiatives and vision. So often, people cannot conceive of things getting better and better. It's why Napoleón Bonaparte said, *"A leader is a dealer in hope."*

But Moses' hope began faltering as well. Leaders are not immune to discouragement. Moses said to God, *"If the Israelites will not listen to me, why would Pharaoh listen to me, since I speak with faltering lips."* (Exodus 6:12) Leaders rarely have instant success. It takes time, patience, and powers of persuasion for a leader to convince followers to embrace the vision articulated by the leader. Leaders must learn to persevere, to overcome personal disappointments and setbacks when their efforts to lead the community forward do not produce the hoped-for result. Moses summoned his courage and returned to Pharaoh.

First Plague: Blood
Moses returned to Pharaoh and demanded: *"Let my people go."* (Exodus 7:16)
Pharaoh responded: *"Pharaoh's heart became hard; he would not listen to Moses and Aaron, just as the Lord had said."* (Exodus 7:22)

Would Moses go back to Pharaoh after being rejected twice? At times, leaders must be understanding and patient, and at other times, forceful and persistent. Leaders must appreciate that different approaches are required for different situations and different constituencies. Note that Moses returned to Pharaoh again.

Second Plague: Frogs
Moses demanded: *"Let my people go."* (Exodus 8:1)
Pharaoh responded: *"When Pharaoh saw that there was relief, he hardened his heart and would not listen to Moses and Aaron, just as the Lord had said."* (Exodus 8:15)

Third Plague: Gnats
Pharaoh responded: *"But Pharaoh's heart was hard and he would not listen."* (Exodus 8:19)

Fourth Plague: Flies
Moses demanded: *"Let my people go."* (Exodus 8:20)
Pharaoh responded: *"But this time also Pharaoh hardened his heart and would not let the people go."* (Exodus 8: 32)

Fifth Plague: On Livestock
Moses demanded: *"Let my people go."* (Exodus 9:1)
Pharaoh responded: *"Yet his heart was unyielding and he would not let the people go."* (Exodus 9:7)

Sixth Plague: Boils
Pharaoh responded: *"But the Lord hardened Pharaoh's heart and he would not listen to Moses and Aaron, just as the Lord had said to Moses."* (Exodus 9:12)

Seventh Plague: Hail

Moses demanded: *"Let my people go."* (Exodus 9:13)

Pharaoh responded: *"When Pharaoh saw that the rain and hail and thunder had stopped, he sinned again: He and his officials hardened their hearts."* (Exodus 9:34)

Eighth Plague: Locusts

Moses demanded: *"Let my people go."* (Exodus 10:4)

Pharaoh responded: *"But the Lord hardened Pharaoh's heart, and he would not let the Israelites go."* (Exodus 10:20)

Ninth Plague: Darkness

Pharaoh responded: *"But the Lord hardened Pharaoh's heart, and he was not willing to let them go. Pharaoh said to Moses, 'Get out of my sight! Make sure you do not appear before me again! The day you see my face you will die.'"* (Exodus 10:27, 28)

Tenth Plague: On the Firstborn

Pharaoh responded: *"Go, worship the Lord as you have requested. Take your flocks and your herds, as you have said, and go. And also bless me."* (Exodus 12:31, 32)

We can see a pattern in these five chapters from Exodus. It's a pattern not difficult to see. Can you see it? It is ***RESISTANCE TO CHANGE!*** Moses experienced resistance from Pharaoh at every step.

But this will not be the only resistance Moses will face. Moses will experience continuous resistance and opposition even from the people he was leading. The story of Israel's journey from bondage in Egypt to the Promise Land is filled with other experiences of resistance. So, expect resistance and do not be surprised by it.

Nicolo Machiavelli, a 15th century philosopher and writer, and a key figure in realist political theory said, *"There is nothing more difficult to take in hand, more perilous to conduct or more uncertain in its success, than to take the lead in the introduction of a new order of things."* So, do not underestimate the challenge of introducing a new vision or initiating change.

EXERCISE: *Your reaction to resistance*

Identify a time in your past when a person or persons resisted an idea you shared. How did you respond? If you can't identify such an experience, reflect on why that is and write your answer below.

_____

_____

_____

_____

_____

_____

_____

EXPOSURE: *Why do people resist change or a new vision?*

I've noticed that young or inexperienced leaders can react to peoples' resistance in one of two ways. Some young or inexperienced leaders, fearing resistance, will avoid leading in any direction where the leader feels that he or she will encounter resistance.

The other reaction to resistance I've observed is when the young or inexperienced leader decides to meet resistance with an equal or greater force (referred to as the Bigger Hammer approach) in order to push the new vision or change forward.

Both of these responses to resistance are ineffective in leading transformational change. They are *REACTIONS* versus an effective *ACTION* to leading change. To effectively lead in introducing a new vision for the future and a new direction, the leader cannot be reactive to people's initial response of resistance.

Begin now to think of resistance as simply *feedback* that effective leaders need in order to ultimately see people embrace change. People respond in different ways to change from passively resisting to outright resistance and conflict. How people respond to the introduction of change is simply their feedback. Consider some of the reasons people resist change, all of which find their root in fear:

Tradition is one of the reasons people in a congregation will resist a new vision or change. Everyone has heard those infamous seven last words of a dying church: "We've always done it this way before." People fear any change that threatens their long-held values.

Uncertainty is another reason people will resist. The status quo represents what is predicable, comfortable and safe. People fear the unknown. A new vision or change represents uncertainty, discomfort, risk and potential danger. Given the choice, people are inclined to choose the comfort of the status quo.

Loss of position is another reason people in a congregation will resist a new vision or change. A new vision or change can be perceived as a threat to a person's position or his influence in a congregation. People fear that, with change, there may not be a place for them.

Loss of control. Some people will perceive a new vision or change as a threat to their control in the congregation.

People's feedback about change is important information for a leader. What you don't know can hurt you as a leader. That's why people's reaction to change—resistance—when understood can be invaluable to a leader. Rather than react to people's fear, it is best for leaders to explore the specific reasons for the resistance, people's fear responses.

Once you understand what is at the root of people's resistance, you can begin to address their concerns and reassure them.

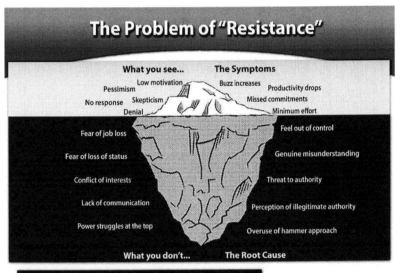

The challenge for the effective change leader will be for him or her not to just identify the symptoms of resistance. The effective leader will want to look below the surface to discern the deeper and larger reasons for the resistance. With this knowledge, the leader can better address the concerns and reassure the individuals of how the new vision or change can enhance the life of the congregation or organization.

Everett M. Rogers was a sociologist best known for originating the diffusion of innovation theory which stated that the individuals in a social system do not adopt an innovation at the same time. Rather, they adopt change over time, so that individuals can be classified into adopter categories on the basis of when they first begin using a new idea. In short, the diffusion of innovation theory holds that **NOT EVERYBODY ACCEPTS CHANGE EQUALLY!**

The diffusion of innovation

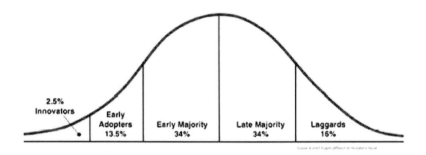

Everett Rogers defines diffusion as the process by which an innovation is communicated through certain channels over time among the members of a social system

Here is a brief description of Rogers' five groups:

Innovators account for 2.5 percent of individuals in a system. Innovators, because they are willing to take risks and able to cope with a high level of uncertainty, are the first individuals to adopt an innovation. Rogers said of innovators,

> *"While an innovator may not be respected by the other members of a local system, the innovator plays an important role in the diffusion process; that of launching the new idea in the system by importing the innovation from outside of the system's boundaries."*

Innovators are the dreamers and the visionaries in your congregation or organization.

Early Adopters account for 13.5 percent. Individuals in this category adopt an innovation after a varying degree of time. They are usually more integrated into the congregation than the innovators and therefore are more trusted. The value of getting early adopters on board with a new vision, according to Rogers is, that *"early adopters decrease uncertainty about a new idea by adopting it."* Early adopters are those members of your congregation or organization who know a good idea when they see it.

Early Majority Adopters account for 34 percent. The early majority adopts new ideas just before the average member of a system. The early majority is the most numerous of the adopter categories, making up one-third of the members of a system. Rogers said of middle adopters:

> *"The early majority may deliberate for some time before completely adopting a new idea. Their innovation-decision period is relatively longer than that of the innovator and the early adopter. They follow with deliberate willingness in adopting innovations, but seldom lead."*

Late Majority Adopters also accounts for 34 percent. The late majority adopts new ideas just after the average member of a system. Like the early majority, the late majority makes up one-third of the members of a system. Regarding those in the late majority group, Rogers said:

> *"Innovations are approached with a skeptical and cautious air, and the late majority do not adopt until most others in their system have done so. The weight of system norms must definitely favor an innovation before the late majority are convinced."*

This will be the last group in a congregation or organization to endorse a new idea.

Laggards/Never Adopters make up the remaining 16 percent. New ideas are seldom, if ever, accepted by this group. These individuals typically have an aversion to change-agents and typically tend to be focused on "traditions." Rogers said of Laggards: *"Laggards tend to be suspicious of innovations and change agents. Their innovation-decision process is relatively lengthy."*

Understanding that **NOT EVERYBODY ACCEPTS CHANGE EQUALLY** is critically important to any leader attempting to introduce change.

Five Implications of the "Diffusion of Innovation" Bell Curve:

1. Accept the reality that not everybody accepts change equally.
2. Realize that not everyone will be happy. Some members may choose to leave.
3. Make innovator and early adopters your allies.
4. The battle is for the middle adopters. Commit your energies to getting middle adopters on board.
5. You don't have to have everyone on board to begin to see change. A critical *"take off point"* is at between 10% and 20% of the system, where a sufficiently large number of people in the congregation have adopted the new vision or change. (Malcolm Gladwell took this idea—the whole notion of innovation diffusion behaving like epidemics—and used it as the foundation of his book *The Tipping Point*.)

EXERCISE: Innovators and Early Adopters

Take a few moments to think about your congregation or organization and begin identifying your allies, the innovators, and the early adopters in your congregation.

1. _____
2. _____
3. _____
4. _____
5. _____
6. _____
7. _____
8. _____

EXPOSURE: *Effective leaders of change*

Leaders of change set the cultural climate in their respective churches or organizations. Look below at the factors that make it more likely that people will be receptive to change:

- ***EFFECTIVE LEADERS OF CHANGE UNDERSTAND THE CHALLENGE OF INTRODUCING CHANGE.***

In my mind, there is no greater leadership challenge than leading change. Significant change is not easy to bring about nor can it happen quickly. In fact, the greater the change, the more communication and the more time will be needed for people to accept and embrace the change. A change leader must possess strength of character, a skill set conducive to leading change, and enormous determination and patience with process. This is all to say that effective leaders understand the high-risk challenge of introducing change in their congregation or organization.

- ***EFFECTIVE LEADERS OF CHANGE DEVELOP A CULTURE OF TRUST.***

Without a high level of trust there will not be full engagement by members of your congregation or organization. You can have a vision for where God is calling you as a congregation, but if the vision caster suffers low credibility, then the success of the change effort is in jeopardy. If people don't believe in the vision caster, they won't believe in the vision. In order to be successful in leading change, a leader must be trustworthy or credible.

James Kouzes and Barry Posner, in their book *Credibility*, write:

> *"Credible leaders set the example for others; they are willing to hold themselves to the same standards as others. Credible leaders go first. They truly walk the talk."* (p. 187)

Credible, trustworthy leaders don't simply have a set of values; they actually live out their values. They do what James 1:22 says. *"Do not merely listen to the word, and so deceive yourselves. Do what it says."*

> *Be careful of your thoughts, for your thoughts become your words; Be careful of your words, for your words become your deeds; Be careful of your deeds, for your deeds become your habits; Be careful of habits, for your habits become your character; Be careful of your character, for your character becomes your destiny.*
>
> —anonymous

- *EFFECTIVE LEADERS OF CHANGE UNDERSTAND THE POWER OF VISION.*

Vision provides people a picture of a final destination and provides them a compelling reason to abandon the status quo. One of the main reasons why change efforts fail is due to lack of God-given vision. People will not give up the comfort and security of the present, and risk everything, unless a compelling vision of where God want to take them, grips their hearts.

- *EFFECTIVE LEADERS OF CHANGE SHOW PEOPLE HOW THE CHANGE WILL BENEFIT THEM.*

Effective leaders of change speak the positive benefits of the change. The vision statement itself should reflect a future where some of the present problems and challenges will be minimized, if not erased, when the vision is realized.

- *EFFECTIVE LEADERS OF CHANGE BOTH UNDERSTAND AND VALUE THE HISTORY OF THE ORGANIZATION.*

One of the most serious mistakes a young or inexperienced leader can make is to be impulsive and move too quickly to introduce change. It can communicate disrespect for the history of the organization. Many of us who have been seminary trained have been taught to exegete the text of Scripture, which is the art of interpreting the meaning of Scripture. Congregational leaders need to learn how to exegete the context or culture they are seeking to lead.

Before you introduce any changes, take time to exegete your context by studying and learning a little bit of the culture of the congregation. *"Don't take the fence down until you know the reason it was put up."* (G. K. Chesterton)

EXPERIENCE: *Time for a little self-evaluation*

Review the factors in a leader that make it more likely that people will be receptive to change. Which one might you need some improvement and specifically what change would need to come in you to be a more effective leader of change?

_____

_____

_____

_____

_____

_____

CHAPTER 7

THE FIRST BIG STEP IN IMPLIMENTING GOD'S VISION

Exodus 12

KEY PRINCIPLE: THE FIRST BIG STEP IN IMPLEMENTING GOD'S VISION IS LEAVING.

> *"Now the length of time the Israelite people lived in Egypt was 430 years. At the end of the 430 years, to the very day, all the Lord's divisions left Egypt."*
> —Exodus 12: 40-41

EXPOSURE: Letting go!

It is not enough to receive God's vision or even cast or communicate God's vision to others. A leader must help people embrace God's vision. This all begins with a first step of letting go. There's a beautiful metaphor for this first step in implementing God's vision. It's the trapeze.

A trapeze is an aerial apparatus commonly found in circus performances. It is a short horizontal bar hung by ropes or metal straps from a support. The trapeze artist knows that in order to be ready for the bar coming her way, she has to let go of the old bar, the one which is currently providing her safety. She knows that there is no safety in holding onto something that doesn't take you where you want to go. She understands that if she wants to take hold of the approaching bar, she has to take the risk and let go of the old bar.

A time came when the Israelites had to leave Egypt. The Israelites had to let go of everything they had known for the past 400 years and take hold of God's new assignment to journey to the Promise Land. *"During the night Pharaoh summoned Moses and Aaron and said, 'Up! Leave my people, you and the Israelites! Go, worship the LORD as you have requested."* (Exodus 12:31) *And the Israelites left!*

Many visions are never embraced because people will not leave or let go of what is, what has been, in order to take hold of what could be. Many congregations will not let go of their past and the way they've always done things. Yet, these congregations envision their lives in a different way; they desperately long for a different experience. But they are resolved to doing the same things they've always done.

 Albert Einstein defined insanity this way: *"Insanity is doing the same thing over and over again, and expecting different results."* If a congregation aspires for a different experience other than the one they presently have, then the congregation must be willing to do things differently, and this all begins by letting go of how things have been done.

 It has been said that a journey of a thousand miles begins with one step. Taking hold of God and what He has invited us to do will feel like an enormous risk. Letting go, leaving, is a huge step toward embracing God's vision for any congregation.

The truth be told, holding on, staying the same has an attraction. Doing things the way we've always done them is familiar to us, predictable, comfortable, and yes, safe. These things sound attractive to people, and left to themselves, without a compelling vision, many people will choose what is familiar, predictable, comfortable, and safe.

Change is not easy and the longer you hold on, the longer you stay, the greater the attraction to stay. The older you become, the older the institution, the harder it is to let go and move in a new direction. I think this is why this little piece of historic data gets tucked into this story: *"Now the length of time the Israelite people lived in Egypt was 430 years. At the end of the 430 years, to the very day, all the LORD's divisions left Egypt."* (Exodus 12:40-41)

God wants to encourage us by the thought, that even after many years doing life the same way, anyone can change. *Israel left!* Their story underscores the principle that *if you want to walk into the Promise Land, you've got to first leave Egypt!*

The principle of leaving, letting go, is found throughout the Word of God. While walking beside the Sea of Galilee, Jesus called two brothers, Simon Peter and Andrew, who were fishing at the time to come and follow him. *"'Come, follow me,' Jesus said, 'and I will make you fishers of men.' At once they left their nets and followed him."* (Matthew 4:19-20)

Going a little further, Jesus met up with two other brothers fishing from their father's boat, James and John. Jesus called them to follow him, *"and immediately they left the boat and their father and followed him."* (Matthew 4:22)

Jesus, in Matthew 19:5, speaks the principle of leaving, of letting go when, in quoting Genesis 2:24, Jesus says, *"For this cause shall a man leave father and mother, and shall cleave to his wife: and they shall be one flesh"* (KJV). In other words, Jesus is saying that if you are going to marry someone, you've got to leave behind being a dependent child of your mother and father.

The story of Peter's walk on the water in Matthew 14:25-32 is another illustration of this leaving, letting go principle. John Ortberg writes about this principle in his popular book, *If You Want to Walk on Water You've Got to Get Out of the Boat*. The boat represents safety, security, comfort, the known, and where Peter's expertise was; he was a fisherman. If Peter had any hope of walking on water toward Jesus, he had to leave the boat. In the same way, if we would hope to do anything significant for God we must get out of the boat, leaving safety, security, comfort and control behind.

The Apostle Paul, in Philippians 3:13-14 says: *"One thing I do: Forgetting what is behind and straining toward what is ahead, I press on toward the goal to win the prize for which God has called me heavenward in Christ Jesus."* Using the metaphor of a runner, the Apostle Paul is saying that if you are going to win a race, let alone compete, you've got to leave the starting blocks.

It makes perfect sense, doesn't it, that if you want to journey to the Promise Land, you can't remain in Egypt? You've got to leave Egypt, Yet, while this principle sounds simple, it is not easy. It requires courage and faith to let go. Holding on is the comfort zone. But be encouraged by this thought: *Starting is half the battle! So, just start the process by letting go.*

EXERCISE: Your experience of letting go

Think about a time when you had to let go or leave something or someone in order to follow God's call. Describe it and the feelings you experienced.

_____

_____

_____

_____

_____

_____

_____

EXPOSURE: *The transition model*

"Letting go" is one stage of the transition process. Any leader of change will want to understand all the stages of the transition model. This model, created by change consultant, William Bridges, helps us understand the process of transitions. (Bridges, *Managing Transitions: Making the Most of Change*, 1991) As with all models, it is not always perfectly sequenced by you or your people. But it does provide markers to know where you or your people are in the transition, and where to lead them next. If you are familiar with the model, then neither you nor the people you are leading are blindsided when it happens.

The main strength of the model is that it focuses on transition, not change. The difference between change and transition is subtle but important. William Bridges writes:

> *"It isn't the changes that do you in, it's the transitions. Change is not the same as transition. Change is situational: the new site, the new boss, the new team roles, the new policy. Transition is the psychological process people go through to come to terms with the new situation. Change is external, transition is internal."* (Bridges, *Managing Transitions: Making the Most of Change*)

Change relates to events outside us, while transition has to do with the inner reorientation, what happens in people's minds, as they go through change. Change can happen very quickly, while transition usually occurs more slowly. Transition is so difficult because it often forces us to re-examine our values, lifestyle, and learning.

It's important to understand how people are feeling as change proceeds, so that you can guide them through it and so that—in the end—they can accept it and support it. The transition model helps a leader to understand how people will feel as you guide them through change.

The model highlights three stages of transition that people go through when they experience change. These are:

Stage 1: Letting Go ⇨

Stage 2: The Neutral Zone ⇨

Stage 3: The New Beginning

Bridges states that people will go through each stage at their own pace. For example, those who are comfortable with the change will likely move ahead to stage three quickly, while others will linger at stages one or two. Additionally, it should be pointed out that people can slip back to a previous stage. Let's examine each of these stages in greater detail.

Stage 1: Letting Go

People enter this initial stage of transition when you first present them with change. This stage is often marked with resistance and emotional upheaval, because people are being forced to let go of something with which they've grown comfortable.

Endings are a time of disengaging ourselves from what we have previously known. It's a time of *"goodbyes,"* along with the emotions associated with loss. Because loss is a factor, it might be helpful to think of transition as a grief process.

We need to understand that, when we lead people in new directions, all kinds of emotions that are part of the grief process will be involved. In this stage of transition, people are likely to experience the following emotions:

- Fear. *"Oh my! What is happening?"*
- Shock and denial. *"I can't believe this is happening!"*
- Anger. *"Why did you lead me this way?"*

- Bargaining. *"Maybe we can go back."*
- Depression. *"There is no going back, is there?"*
- Acceptance. *"I am excited about this new direction!"*

In order to embrace something new, you must accept that something is ending. If you, as a leader, don't acknowledge the emotions of grief that accompany transition, and emotions that you will have as you go through in your own transitions, you'll likely encounter resistance through the entire change process.

Stage 2: The Neutral Zone

In this stage, people affected by the change are often confused, uncertain, and impatient. Depending on how well they're managing the transition, they may also experience a higher workload as they get used to new systems and new ways of doing things. Think of this phase as the bridge between the old and the new; in some ways, people will still be attached to the old, while they are also trying to adapt to the new.

In the neutral zone, people can experience the following emotions:

- Resentment towards the changes. *"I am really not happy about some of these changes! I didn't think it was going to turn out this way!"*
- Low morale and low productivity. *"This is harder than I thought and is probably going to take longer than I thought."*
- Anxiety about their role, status or identity. *"I don't know where I fit in and I don't think anyone appreciates what I've done."*
- Skepticism about the change initiative. *"I'm not sure we are going to pull this off and maybe the way we used to do it is really not that bad"*

Despite these emotions, this stage can also be characterized by great creativity, innovation, and renewal. This is a great time to encourage people to try new ways of thinking or working.

Stage 3: The New Beginning

The last transition stage is a time of acceptance and energy. People have begun to embrace the change initiative. They're building the skills and confidence they need to work successfully in the new way, and they're starting to see early wins from their efforts.

At this stage, people are likely to experience:

- High energy. *"This is an amazing adventure!"*
- Openness to learning. *"I'm learning something every day!"*
- Renewed commitment to the group or their role. *"Whatever the challenge, I'm up for it! We've got a great team!"*

EXERCISE: *Transitional model quiz*

1. The transitional model has _____ stages.
2. The stages are: _____, _____ and _____.
3. Because transition involves loss, it is helpful to think of transition as a _____ process.
4. In the neutral zone people are often confused, uncertain, and _____.
5. In stage three people begin to embrace the _____ initiative.

EXPOSURE: *Leading people through transition*

If you want to lead people through change successfully, then transitions will take a lot of energy and will require a lot of your attention. Do not shortchange the process. Don't get impatient or try to push people through to stage three; instead, do what you can to lead them positively and sensitively through each stage of the transition process. If the transition is managed poorly, toxic behavior can be seeded in the congregation and linger for years. Grief is a process that takes time, and everyone's timing is different.

Leading People through Stage One

During stage one, it's important to accept people's initial resistance, and understand their grief emotions as a normal part of the process. Allow people time to accept the change and try to get everyone to talk about what they're feeling as they go through the transition. In these conversations, make sure that you listen empathetically and communicate openly about what's going to happen. Emphasize how the grief process is a normal process for anyone moving in a new direction.

The most significant, underlying emotion people will have is the emotion of fear. Learn to help people identify their specific fears by asking processing questions such as:

- What most concerns you or causes you to fear the change?
- Between 0 and 10, what is your level of fear?
- What do you imagine could reduce your fear?

The first response to any God-size vision is generally fear which is the greatest enemy of change. So, help people identify their specific fear. Once you help people identify their fear, challenge people to exercise God-size faith rather than give in to fear. Faith is not the absence of fear but courage in the face of fear.

I think that God says *"fear not"* so often because fear is the number one reason people avoid doing what God asks them to do. We need to be reminded as leaders, that God has called us to *"fear not"* and we need to remind people we are leading to *"fear not."* Lloyd Ogilvie notes that there are 366 *"fear not"* verses in the Bible—one for every day including one for leap year.

During stage one, be sure to communicate and emphasize how the future will be preferred to how things have been. Reassure the congregation that, as they take steps, they will eventually get there together. People often fear what they don't understand, so the more you can educate them about the process and the positive future, and communicate how taking appropriate steps will achieve the vision, the more likely they are to move on to the next stage.

Above all, be patient with the process. Leading change successfully requires a leader who is in it for the *"long haul."* Remember, it took God only one night to get the Israelites out of Egypt, but it took forty years for God to get Egypt out of the Israelites.

Leading People through Stage Two

Your guidance as a leader is incredibly important as people go through this neutral period. This can be an uncomfortable time for the congregation because it will feel like they are traveling into "no man's land." This will be new territory for everyone.

The neutral zone feels like swinging between the trapezes. It is a difficult place to be emotionally, and the very real temptation will be to want to go back; this could happen for some of your people. This is why Moses, on countless occasions, had to deal with the people wanting to return to Egypt. Change, even change towards a more positive future, can be difficult and scary.

Because people might feel a bit lost, provide them with a solid sense of direction. At stage two, it will be important for the congregation to have short-term goals or milestones towards the vision. These short-term goals are important, so that people can experience some early wins which will help to increase their motivation as well as giving everyone a positive perception of the change effort. Early short-term wins are incredibly important during stage two in creating confidence and positive energy for change.

During this stage, the congregation will need the leader and leadership team to be cheerleaders, encouraging the congregation through their fear, anger, and reluctance to take the next step. Here is an encouraging thought that comes from Moses' leadership journal. *"By day the LORD went ahead of them in a pillar of cloud to guide them on their way and by night in a pillar of fire to give them light, so that they could travel by day or night."* (Exodus 13:21)

Underline the phrase: *"the Lord went ahead of them."* This is a tremendously encouraging thought for any leader or congregation. God will not invite you to go anywhere that God has not gone first. God goes ahead of you! Isn't that encouraging?

A two-year-old little girl stands on the side of the pool. *"Jump!"* her father says with open arms. *"Don't be afraid. You can trust me. I won't let you fall. Jump!"*

She is in that moment a bundle of inner conflict. On the one hand, everything inside her is screaming stay put. The water is deep, cold and dangerous. She has never done this before. She can't swim. What if something goes wrong? Bad things could happen.

On the other hand, that is her daddy in the water. He is bigger and stronger than she is and hasn't been anything but trustworthy up to this point in her life. He exudes confidence in her. The battle is between fear and trust. Trust says, *"Jump!"* Fear says, *"Hold on!"* She cannot stay on the side of the pool forever. Eventually she comes to a decision. She jumps!

The spiritual leader and leadership team must model trust and confidence in the One who calls us to *"Jump!"* and invite others to trust in the One who will not invite us to go anywhere that He has not gone first. So, as you lead change, stay connected to your people to encourage them to talk about what they are feeling, and to provide them feedback on the progress they are making.

Moses had many conversations with the Israelites. Early in their journey to the Promise Land we read that: *"They were terrified and cried out to the LORD. They said to Moses, "Was it because there were no graves in Egypt that you brought us to the desert to die? What have you done to us by bringing us out of Egypt? Didn't we say to you in Egypt, 'Leave us alone; let us serve the Egyptians'? It would have been better for us to serve the Egyptians than to die in the desert!"* (Exodus 14:10-12)

Frustration, fear, and even anger are not unusual emotions during change initiatives. The Israelites became fear-filled and angry with Moses because they felt he had led them from the *comfort zone* of Egypt to the *groan zone* of the desert. They tried to negotiate and bargain with Moses to return to Egypt because he had led them out of the familiarity and security of Egypt. Leaders of change must become comfortable with feelings of anger as normal feelings during a change process and courageously lead forward.

Leading People through Stage Three

As people begin to adopt the change, it's essential that you help them sustain their commitment to the new direction. Be sure to take time to celebrate the change you've all gone through and reward your team for all their hard work. Regularly highlight stories of success brought about by the change. Any progress and the celebration that accompanies it will go a long way to building momentum. As you celebrate the new, be sure to honor the past.

However, do not become too complacent—remember that not everyone will reach this stage at the same time, and also remember that people can slip back to previous stages if they think that the change isn't working. Just continue to reinforce the change by anchoring the change to embraced values and goals that are consistent with God's vision for the congregation.

Henri Nouwen, priest and author, just before he died, wrote about a good friend of his, a trapeze artist. This friend explained that there is a very special relationship between the flyer and the catcher. (I would hope so. If I was a flyer, I would want to be a very good friend of the catcher. I would work very hard at making sure there was no animosity between me and my catcher friend. I would want the catcher to like me a lot.)

As the flyer is swinging high above the crowd, the moment comes when he lets go of the trapeze, when he arcs out into the air. For that moment, which must feel like eternity, the flyer is suspended in nothingness. It is too late to reach back for the trapeze. There is no going back now. However, it is too soon to be grasped by the one who will catch him. In that moment, his job is to be still and as motionless as he can.

You see, *"The flyer must never catch the catcher,"* the trapeze artist told Nouwen. *"He must wait in absolute trust. The catcher will catch him. But he must wait. His job is not to flail about in anxiety. In fact, if he does, it could kill him. His job is to be still; to wait. And to wait is the hardest job of all."*

We must be willing to let go of whatever God has called us to let go of. When we do, we may not feel God's hand catching us immediately. What is critical is that we wait in absolute trust because He will be there to catch us!

The journey of the Israelites began with the first step of leaving, which is no small step. Their journey began when *"the people took their dough before the yeast was added, and carried it on their shoulders in kneading troughs wrapped in clothing. The Israelites did as Moses instructed and asked the Egyptians for articles of silver and gold and for clothing. The LORD had made the Egyptians favorably disposed toward the people, and they gave them what they asked for; so they plundered the Egyptians. The Israelites journeyed from Rameses to Succoth."* (Exodus 12:34-37)

The people of Israel moved quickly out of Egypt at the urging of the Egyptians. They moved so quickly that they didn't take time to add yeast to their dough. But the important thing is that they left. Leaving is a HUGE step!

The first law of Newton's law of motion states that a body at rest tends to stay at rest unless acted upon by another force. What does this have to do with leading your congregation toward God's vision? Consider that a congregation has been motionless for a long time, will not easily move, and that any motion away from motionlessness ought to be encouraged and celebrated.

The first motion away from motionlessness may look awkward and will likely not be perfect. But encourage it and celebrate it anyway, because before you can create movement toward God's vision, let alone momentum, you first have to have any kind of motion or movement.

So, are you ready? What vision has God called you to take hold of? What journey in your life has been taking so long because you are holding on to the past trapeze? Are you ready to let go? *ONE! TWO! THREE! LET GO!*

EXPERIENCE: Helping your congregation let go

Reflect on the congregation you are leading. What are some of the things your congregation will be required to let go of in order take hold of God's vision? Once you've identified these things, write what you would say to encourage these members to *"let go."* In groups of three or four, share your responses and seek feedback on how you could encourage even more effectively.

_____

_____

_____

_____

_____

_____

_____

_____

_____

_____

_____

_____

_____

_____

_____

_____

_____

_____

CHAPTER 8

FURTHER STEPS IN LEADING TOWARD GOD'S VISION

Exodus 12 & 13

KEY PRINCIPLE: IMPLEMENTING GOD'S VISION REQUIRES A VISION PATH

"My Lord knows the way through the wilderness,
All I have to do is follow."
—Children's Gospel Song

EXPOSURE: Not a step, but a succession of steps

Why did it take Moses forty years to lead the people of Israel from Egypt to the Promise Land, a short journey from Egypt to Canaan by the most direct route?

The joke goes: *Why did it take Moses forty years to lead the people of Israel from Egypt to the Promise Land, a journey that could have been accomplished in less than two weeks?* The answer: *Like most men, Moses would not ask for directions.*

Forty years is a long time. And those forty years weren't easy years. The truth is leading transformational change is not easy and will take you longer than you think. Often, efforts to bring major change in a congregation or organization fail. Not only is there failure, but I have talked to countless pastors who lost their jobs in the process of introducing change. Do not miss this, or dismiss this:

> *Leading transformation change is a high-risk deal!*

Failure in transformation efforts usually are associated with not understanding the complexity and difficulty in producing change. The young and inexperienced leader can come to think that transformational change requires simply the casting of a clear and compelling vision and the leader's abilities of persuasion. Young and inexperienced leaders assume that people will immediately embrace the vision and lock arms as they walk together toward the vision.

Leading change is much more complicated and challenging than this. Developing a vision is one step in a long process toward achieving the vision. What leaders need to understand, given the complexity and difficulty of producing change, is that leading change is a *process* that requires what I call, *"a vision path."*

John Kotter is a professor of leadership at Harvard Business School, an author of seven best-selling books, and is a frequent speaker at top management meetings around the world. In his book, *Leading Change*, Kotter identifies eight stages or steps for leading transformational change. These eight steps provide a *vison path* that can help the leader navigate the challenges of introducing change. The eight-stage process, which we will look at in detail in this chapter, includes these stages or steps:

1. Establish a Sense of Urgency
2. Create a Guiding Coalition
3. Develop a Vision and Strategy
4. Communicate the Change Vision
5. Empower Members for Broad-Based Action
6. Generate Short-Term Wins
7. Consolidate Gains and Produce More Change
8. Anchor New Approaches in the Culture

1.   ESTABLISH A SENSE OF URGENCY.

This sign was once seen beside a major dirt road in the Australian outback:

> *"Choose your rut carefully! You will be in it for the next 200 miles."*

Many congregations and organizations find themselves in a comfortable rut for years, the rut of diminishing vitality, declining and aging membership and loss of a sense of mission. Without a sense of urgency, congregations and organizations often resign themselves to the comfortable rut.

What is needed to get congregations and organizations to consider leaving the rut is what John Kotter calls *"a sense of urgency."* Kotter writes:

> *"By far the biggest mistake people make when trying to change organizations is to plunge ahead without establishing a high enough sense of urgency in fellow managers and employees. This error is fatal because transformations always fail to achieve their objective when complacency levels are high."* (Kotter, *Leading Change*, p. 4)

The first step to getting people to move toward God's vision, is to create a sense of urgency. One of the key reasons why change efforts fail is a lack of a sense of urgency. If people do not see the need for change and the importance of acting immediately, people will not change. If there is complacency around the status quo and little or no discontent with the status quo, then it will be quite challenging to lead in changing the situation.

Someone once said, *"People don't always change when they see the light as much as when they feel the heat."* If the leader cannot help people see the need to change— better, feel the need to change—they will not change. One of the roles of an effective leader of change is to help others see and feel the need for change and the importance of acting immediately.

A great sense of urgency surrounded the Israelites leaving Egypt. The Israelites left Egypt in a hurry. *"During the night Pharaoh summoned Moses and Aaron and said, 'Up! Leave my people, you and the Israelites! Go, worship the LORD as you have requested. Take your flocks and herds, as you have said, and go. And also bless me.' The Egyptians urged the people to <u>hurry and leave</u> the country. 'For otherwise,' they said, 'we will all die!'"* (Exodus 12:31-33) The sense of urgency for Pharaoh and the Israelites was created by the crisis of the tenth plague, the death of every first-born in Egypt that had not come under the blood painted on doorposts.

Sometimes a sense of urgency will be created by a crisis in a congregation. A crisis will often reveal problems and issues in the congregation that need to be addressed. It is the wise leader who will use a crisis to dramatize the need for change in the congregation.

Without an immediate crisis, a skilled change leader can create a sense of urgency by helping the congregation to see what will likely happen in the future if the congregation fails to act. The leader can use research and the congregation's own data to help the congregation see, for example, that if the congregation is not more successful in reaching the community with the Gospel and seeing people incorporated into the life of the church they will continue to decline. Or, for example, if the congregation is not more successful in reaching younger people, they will continue to grow older as a congregation and their future will be in jeopardy.

Sometimes a sense of urgency can be created by helping the congregation see the vitality of the New Testament church reaching the world with the claims of the Gospel as compared to the congregation's own lack of vitality and its lethargic commitment to the mission of Christ. This is essentially what many of the Biblical prophets were doing when they communicated God's vision for God's people as opposed to the way they were presently living, and calling for repentance (change), without which they could expect disaster.

2.   CREATE A GUIDING COALITION.

Major change is often said to be impossible unless the pastor of the congregation or the head of the organization is an active supporter. Having the pastor or head of the organization on board is essential for change to occur. But having only the pastor or only the head of the organization on board, is insufficient to bring about transformational change.

Kotter calls for a guiding coalition, or what I called a *"vision team"* back in Chapter 5: *Better Together*. Transformational change requires a team. One of the many reasons transformational change fails to happen is that a leader will try to go it alone. Look again at *Better Together* to see how to select a vision team.

3.   DEVELOP A VISION AND STRATEGY

Vision provides people a picture of the final destination and provides them a compelling reason to abandon the status quo. One of the main reasons why change efforts fail is due to a lack of God-given vision. People will not give up the comfort and security of the present, and risk everything, unless a compelling vision grips their hearts.

Review Chapter 3: *The Power of Vision*. Vision plays a key role in producing transformational change by helping to direct, align and inspire movement toward God's vision.

4.   COMMUNICATE THE CHANGE VISION

Another reason change efforts fail is under-communication of the vision. John Kotter make the point that one of the reasons why change efforts fail is under-communicating the vision by a factor of 10. (or 100 or even 1,000) He writes that we need to make the communication of vision redundant, simple, visual, emotional, logical and repetitious. (John P. Kotter, *Leading Change, p.9*)

Many leaders, when asked if they regularly communicate the vision will answer, *"Yes"* because we think we've already spoken the vison several times. But none of us casts vision enough! Bill Hybels nails it when he says, *"Vision leaks!"* (Bill Hybels, *Axiom: Powerful Leadership Proverbs*) Hybels, in speaking about *"vision leak,"* is pointing out the reality that people tend to forget the vision that was cast just months ago. For vision to stick, the vision must be cast over and over and over and over.

A mistake leaders can make is to forget that while the leader and the vision team have been discussing the vision for some time, the rest of the congregation has not been a part of the intense discussion, and soul-searching process. So, the vision needs to be communicated often for the congregation to embrace it. Rick Warren echoes this view when he says, *"Vision and purpose must be restated every twenty-six days to keep the church moving in the right direction."* (Rick Warren, *The Purpose Driven Church*)

Vision must be communicated continuously because vision clarifies the direction we are heading. Vision motivates by giving a picture of a preferable future destination. Vision focuses our energy and our effort on the steps we need to take to achieve the vision. So, if you are trying to lead others to move toward God's vision for your congregation or organization, make sure you communicate the vision often to achieve understanding and buy-in.

EXERCISE: How often are you communicating vision?

How often do you communicate the vision to your congregation or organization? If you have not identified God's vision for you congregation or organization, how often do you communicate where you hope to lead your congregation or organization?

Weekly   _____
Monthly   _____
Quarterly   _____
Annually   _____
Rarely   _____
Never   _____

5 Ways to Communicate the Vision

Leaders make the mistake to think that because they've spoken the vision several times, the congregation understands it and has embraced it. The reality is that people absorb only a small portion of what they hear. Vision must be communicated continuously, but vision must also be communicated in more than one way. Communicating the vision in a variety of ways makes it more likely that people will catch God's vision and buy into the vision. Here are five ways:

Communicate the vision by embodying it. One of the first, and I believe the most important, ways a leader communicates vision is by embodying it. The leader needs to personify the vision and live it out. In fact, nothing will compromise the vision more quickly than leadership that lacks the integrity of living out the very vision the leader espouses.

Communicate the vision one-on-one. A second way to communicate the vision is having one-on-one conversations, beginning with key leaders and influencers in the church. An effective vision-casting leader will not only communicate the vision to the crowd, but will also take the time to sit down with key influencers to personally and passionately share the vision that has gripped his or her heart and ask for commitment.

Communicate the vision by going public. Many young and inexperienced leaders will make the mistake of going public with the vision before they themselves embody it and have key leaders and influencers on board. However, a time comes when the leader needs to communicate God's vision to the entire congregation. Annually, usually in January, I presented a series of messages on vision where I tried to communicate the vision for our congregation in a fresh and creative way.

Communicate the vision visually. Research shows that people generally remember only 10% of what they read. They remember 20% of what they hear and 30% of what they see. Retention is increased to 50% if they hear and see something, as in watching a movie or a demonstration. Vision itself is visual; even more reason for leaders to communicate the vision in ways that people can actually see it through pictures, video, drama, or modeling.

Communicate the vision by celebrating. This is, in fact, what the Passover was for the Israelites; the Passover was a celebration of God's deliverance from bondage in Egypt to occupy the Promise Land. Put mile markers along the way, and celebrate! What motivates and keeps people on the journey toward the vision is a sense of hope that they're making progress and that they're going to get there someday.

It's important to celebrate along the way, not just at the end. Look for every opportunity to celebrate. When was the last time, you as a leader, led a celebration for progress made toward the vision, not just for reaching the destination?

EXERCISE: Communicating the vision

Think of as many ways as you can to communicate the vision, especially visual communication. Consider your small groups, videos, dramas website, and art, etc.

List the various ways you could communicate God's vision to your congregation or organization.

_____

_____

_____

_____

_____

_____

_____

5.   EMPOWER MEMBERS FOR BROAD-BASED ACTION

The greater the number of people who understand the vision and embrace the vision, the greater your critical mass, the more likely you will be successful leading a change effort toward a new vision. This principle sounds like common sense, yet it is amazing to me how few leaders think strategically about creating critical mass in leading significant change.

When you begin to look into creating a critical mass of people who would support the change effort toward the new vision, the leader needs to look within the congregation for those who trust the leader, as well as, other members of the congregation who have a relatively high level of trust. Alan Nelson and Gene Appel, in their book, *How to Change Your Church (without killing it)*, remind us that leadership is basically relational banking, whereby certain individuals with influence are entrusted by others to lead them well.

Begin thinking of the congregation as comprised of circles of trust, circles of influence. Ask the following questions:

- As the *pastor-leader* of the congregation, who is in my circle of influence? Do those in my circle of influence understand the vision and have they embraced it? If there is anyone who hasn't embraced the vision, is there someone else they highly trust who could help them understand and embrace the vision?

- The *official board*— whether it is the elder board, the board of deacons or the board of directors— represents a circle of trust and influence in any congregation. Do the members of the official board understand the vision and have they embraced it? If there is anyone on the official board who hasn't, is there someone else they highly trust who could help them understand and embrace the vision?

- Who are the *key influencers* in the congregation, beyond the board, who have a high level of trust in the congregation and therefore influence? Do these influencers understand the vision and have they embraced it? Which groups are these influencers likely to influence? If there is anyone in those circles who hasn't embraced the vision, is there someone else they highly trust who could help them understand and embrace the vision?

- Are there *"gatekeepers"* in the congregation who, while they may not have an official role, the congregation listens to what they say? Who is most likely to listen to them?

- Are there *influencers in the congregation who might be opposed to the changes* and the new vision? Is there someone else they highly trust who could help them understand and embrace the vision?

The key to building critical mass is getting your key influencers on your team with the change effort toward the new vision.

EXERCISE: *Circles of influence*

Identify the influencers in your congregation and write their names in the appropriate circles.

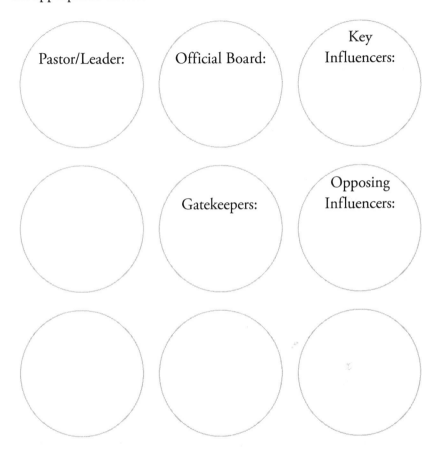

Once you have identified your key influencers, empower them to take action toward the vision. Empower *them by your encouragement. It is so easy to become discouraged!* A leader can fuel movement toward God's vision by his or her encouragement. Encouragement is needed all along the journey, not just at the beginning to get things started, but continuously so that movement is sustained and momentum is built. Here are several ways you can encourage the people you are leading.

You encourage people by believing in them. When it comes to believing in themselves, some people are agnostics. Do you want to be an encourager of people? Do you want to help people make progress toward the vision God has for them? Here is the key to being a great encourager: You encourage others when you believe in them *BEFORE* they believe in themselves!

Encouragement is not needed *after* someone believes in himself or herself. Encouragement is needed *before* a person believes in himself or herself, when the person might seriously doubt whether he or she can do it. It is easy to believe in people after they succeed. The key is believing in people before they succeed.

There was a boy named Tommy who had a particularly hard time in school. He continually asked questions, and he never could quite keep up. It seemed that he failed every time he tried something. His teacher finally gave up on him and told his mother that he could not learn and would never amount to much. But Tommy's mother was an encourager. She believed in him. She taught him at home, and each time he failed, she gave him hope and encouraged him to keep trying. Whatever happened to Tommy? He became an inventor, eventually holding more than one thousand patents, including those for the phonograph and the first commercially practical incandescent electric light bulb. You know him as the inventor Thomas Alva Edison. When people have someone who believes in them, there is no telling what they can accomplish. (*Building Your Mate's Self-Esteem*, Dennis Rainey and Barbara Rainey)

You encourage by your words. People need to hear words of encouragement like:

"Good job!"
"You were awesome!"
"You almost had it! Next time you will!"
"I love watching you lead!"
"Don't give up; keep trying. You'll get it!"

Transitions, going through change, can create insecurity. Congregations, moving through major change, especially need to hear words of encouragement from their leaders!

Perhaps the most powerful way you can encourage is this: **encourage by your presence**. God provided the Israelites a leader who would walk before them. The presence of a leader is important.

The story is told of General George Washington, the first President of the United States, how he once rode along his lines and saw his exhausted men digging trenches – dismounted, removed his coat, rolled up his sleeves, grabbed a pick and began digging with the men. He was, quite literally, in the trenches with his men. The pure inspiration this act engendered among the rank-and-file was immeasurable, which is why the story has survived to this day. Encourage others in every way but especially by your presence!

God encouraged Israel by providing them His presence. *"By day the LORD went ahead of them in a pillar of cloud to guide them on their way and by night in a pillar of fire to give them light, so that they could travel by day or night."* (Exodus 13:21)

As a leader, be encouraged by the fact that God does not invite you to go where He does not go first! Encourage your people by this truth and encourage people by your own presence.

6. GENERATE SHORT-TERM WINS

Early, short-term wins are so very important to keeping the congregation or organization moving toward the vision because they build confidence and build momentum to keep going on. Alternatively, early stalls or failures will challenge the congregation's confidence and disrupt momentum.

Very early in the journey of Moses and the Israelites, God gave them short-term wins. We read in Exodus 12:36, *"The LORD had made the Egyptians favorably disposed toward the people."* In other words, God greased the skids to make the course for Moses and the Israelites a little easier.

If you want to build movement and momentum, remove as many barriers as possible for members of your congregation as they begin to take action. It is not easy starting toward a new direction. It is so easy to become discouraged. Any little barrier can slow down movement or derail it and lead to giving up. So, if you want to build movement and momentum in the people you are trying to lead, remove unnecessary barriers.

Another example of God providing a short-term success is found in Exodus 13:17-18 by guiding the Israelites away from a potential early loss. *"When Pharaoh let the people go, God did not lead them on the road through the Philistine country, though that was shorter. For God said, 'If they face war, they might change their minds and return to Egypt.' So God led the people around by the desert road toward the Red Sea."* Interesting, isn't it?

Why do you think God led the Israelites on this circuitous route to the Promise Land? Could it be that God did not want the Israelites to become discouraged by being defeated by the mighty Philistines? The Israelites were not warriors. They had been slaves for over 400 years. Later, after they had gained confidence, they would end up battling the Philistines and defeating them. Early wins are critically important. So, make every effort to create opportunity for early short-term wins, while avoiding early losses.

One other early short-term win for Moses and the people of Israel was the remarkable and miraculous parting of the sea and the total defeat of Pharaoh and his army as God turned back the water and all the Egyptians were destroyed. Do you think it built their confidence and encouraged them to go on? Of course it did! Exodus 14:31 says, *"When the Israelites saw the great power the LORD displayed against the Egyptians, the people feared the LORD and put their trust in him and in Moses his servant."*

When we follow God and His vision, God allows us to experience victories. The reason God allows us to experience these *"wins"* is so that our confidence and faith in Him grow. God wants our confidence and faith in Him to grow so that we continue to pursue Him and His vision for our lives.

If you want to encourage movement toward God's vision and build momentum, create opportunities for the congregation to experience early short-term wins. On the way toward the vision, create short term goals that can be successfully accomplished and then celebrated. Create opportunities for some visible, unambiguous successes as soon as possible! What these early wins do is build confidence to be able to go after the next goal, and then the next. Success builds confidence that we can be successful the next time. John Kotter writes:

> *"Creating short-term wins is different from hoping for short-term wins. The latter is passive, the former active. In a successful transformation, managers actively look for ways to obtain clear performance improvements, establish goals in the yearly planning system, achieve these objectives, and reward the people involved with recognition, promotions or money."* (Kotter, Leading Change, p. 11)

Creating short-term wins will require some strategic thinking and planning. Admittedly, strategic thinking and planning aren't as exciting as active involvement. Sometimes leadership in a congregation will try to avoid the important step of strategic planning. I believe the reason for this is that planning is hard work. Others avoid strategic planning because they argue, *"We prefer to not rely on human plans, but to operate by faith."* The truth is good planning is an exercise in faith.

Chuck Swindoll in his delightful little book, *Hand Me Another Brick*, where he chronicles the leadership of Nehemiah, writes:

> *"It is of great concern to me that so many people who undertake some project in the Lord's work enter without careful planning. They abruptly begin without thinking through questions such as: 'Where will this lead us? How can I express this in clear, unmistakable, concrete terms? What are the costs, the objectives, the possible pitfalls? What process should be used?' I could name a number of individuals and families who entered the ministry with enthusiasm but later dropped out because they had not considered the cost. The most disillusioned people I know are those in the Lord's work who are paying the price of not thinking through their plans."*

Strategic planning should be covered by prayer. Prayer and planning must go hand in hand. Proverbs 16:3 counsels us to *"commit to the LORD whatever you do, and your plans will succeed."* We need to heed the wisdom of Proverbs 19:21 that says, *"Many are the plans in a man's heart, but it is the LORD's purpose that prevails."* Prayer must permeate every aspect of the planning process so that our plans align with God's purpose.

Begin strategic planning early in the process before you take big actions. You've undoubtedly heard the wise builder's advice to *"Measure twice; cut once."* Jesus reminds us of the wisdom of the builder who, before he saws a board or drives a nail, will *"sit down and estimate the cost to see if he has enough money to complete it."* (Luke 14:28) Unfortunately, I've seen too many congregations engage in strategic thinking only after they've acted; they're thinking about how to get themselves out of the mess they've created.

Create opportunities for short-term wins by setting goals that are in alignment with God's vison for your church. Let's look at what is commonly referred to as S.M.A.R.T. goals. How do you create S.M.A.R.T. goals? Establish goals that are:

Specific: Not general but clearly specific that there would be no doubt when you reached it.

Measurable: Clear about how much or how many.

Attainable: Not be theoretical, but achievable.

Realistic: Representing an objective toward which you are both *willing* and *able* to work.

Timely: Grounded within a time frame; not *"someday"* but *"when exactly?*

What we are doing when we establish S.M.A.R.T. goals is creating opportunity for people to *"win."* And when the people accomplish a goal, be sure to celebration the *"win."*

7.   CONSOLIDATE GAINS and PRODUCE MORE CHANGE

Step seven has to do with creating momentum. John Maxwell writes, *"Momentum is the greatest of all change agents."* (Maxwell, *Developing the Leaders Around You*) What is momentum?

Momentum is a commonly used term in sports. A team that has a lot of momentum is really *on the move* and is going to be *hard to stop*. A sports announcer will say, *"Going into the second half of the season, the Santiago de Cuba baseball team has the momentum."* The newspaper headlines will announce *"Havana Baseball team Gaining Momentum."* A coach, attempting to *pump* up his team at half-time, will say, *"You have the momentum; the critical need now is that you use that momentum and bury them in this third quarter."*

You can literally feel momentum change in a game, can't you? Momentum is a *game changer*. In leadership, leaders cannot afford to overlook the importance of momentum. John Maxwell in his book *Developing the Leaders Around You*, writes:

> With momentum…   *leaders look better than they actually are.*
> With momentum…   *followers increase their performance.*
> Without momentum…   *leaders look worse than they actually are.*
> Without momentum…   *followers decrease their performance.*

Momentum is the greatest of all change agents… To maximize the value of momentum, leaders must: (1) develop an appreciation for it early; (2) know the key ingredients of it immediately; and (3) pour resources into it always.

The word *momentum* is also a term in the world of physics, where momentum refers to the quantity of motion that an object has. If an object is in motion (*on the move*) then it has *momentum.* In physics, *momentum* is defined as *"mass in motion."* All objects have mass; so if an object is moving, then it has momentum.

The amount of momentum that an object has is dependent upon two variables: how much *stuff* is moving (mass) and how fast the *stuff* is moving (velocity). In terms of an equation, the momentum of an object is equal to the mass of the object times the velocity of the object. In physics, the symbol for the quantity momentum is the lower case **p.** In physics the equation can be written as . . .

$$p = mv$$

. . . where **m** is the mass and **v** is the velocity. The equation illustrates that momentum is directly proportional to an object's mass and directly proportional to the object's velocity.

Alright, how does this discussion relate to momentum in leadership and specifically momentum as it relates to leading change? In leadership, just as in the world of physics, momentum involves two critical ingredients: mass and velocity.

When it comes to leading change, critical mass has to do with the number of people who understand the vision and have embraced the vision. The more people who understand and embrace the vision, the greater is the potential for motion and momentum. This is why, earlier in the book, I encouraged you to get as many of your key influencers on board with the vision as early as possible in the process.

Velocity, as it relates to leading change, has to do with the amount and speed of motion or movement toward the vision. For leaders to build momentum, leaders need to think in terms of increasing not only the critical mass, but also the speed of change. The speed of change increases, as the leader empowers influencers for broad-based action.

EXERCISE: Momentum Quiz

John Maxwell says that *"momentum is the _____ of all change agents."*

Momentum involves two critical ingredients: _____ and _____.

Mass in a congregation has to do with _____
_____.

Velocity in a congregation has to do with _____
_____.

8.   ANCHOR NEW APPROACHES in the CULTURE

John Kotter writes: *"In the final analysis, change sticks only when it becomes 'the way we do things around here,' when it seeps into the very bloodstream of the work unit or corporate body. Until new behaviors are rooted in social norms and shared values, they are always subject to degradation as soon as the pressures associated with a change effort are removed."* (John Kotter, Leading Change, p. 14)

The drift of people will not be forward toward the vision, but back toward the familiar, the comfortable, and what is easy. John Kotter warns, *"Resistance always waits to reassert itself."* (*Leading Change*, p. 132) It's so true!

How many times did the Israelites want to return to Egypt? How many times did the people return to old patterns? How many times during their journey did the people revert to behaviors of their former lives as slaves?

For vision to be fully embraced and for transformational change to stick, the leader must anchor the changes in the culture or mindset of the congregation or organization. How is this done?

How was the new identity of the people and new way they were to live anchored in the culture through Moses' leadership? In reading Moses' leadership story, you and I can see how their new identity and new ways got anchored in the culture by several ways.

- Their new identity and new ways got anchored in the vision of a Promise Land, a vision that was continually repeated. The land that God had promised to His people was, and always will be, an anchor for God's people.
- Their new identity and new ways got anchored in the celebration of the Passover meal where the people were continually reminded how they had been delivered, what they had been delivered from, and what they had been delivered to. Stories have power and the story of the night when they were delivered by the blood (Passover) was recited again and again, even to this day.
- Their new identity and new ways got anchored by the commandments of God which reflected His heart and the

community values. These commandments were understood as the very Word of God to them that was to guide them in all matters.

What can you and I learn from Moses' leadership about anchors for transformational change? Consider the following four anchors:

- Vision, when it is continually communicated, can serve as an anchor.
- What we celebrate can serve as an anchor of the community.
- What we regularly repeat or practice can be an anchor.
- Community values can serve as an anchor for the community.

EXERCISE: Anchors

What would the average member say is the vision of your congregation?

_____

_____

_____

_____

What are two things your congregation celebrates annually?

_____

_____

_____

_____

What are five practices that get repeated regularly in your congregation?

_____

_____

_____

_____

What are three things your congregation really values?

_____

_____

_____

_____

EXPERIENCE: *All aboard*

Participants are required to build a *"boat"* using pieces of wood, mats, chairs, or any other material available, and then all participants must stand on the *"boat"* at once. As pieces of the boat are removed, the team must endeavor to occupy the ever-diminishing space as best they can. This activity helps to encourage communication, problem solving and critical thinking.

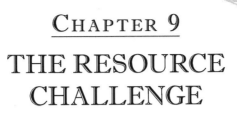

CHAPTER 9

THE RESOURCE CHALLENGE

Exodus 13-18

KEY PRINCIPLE: WHERE GOD GUIDES, GOD PROVIDES!

"My God will meet all your needs according to his glorious riches in Christ Jesus."
—Philippians 4:19

EXPOSURE: God is our provider

As you lead toward God's vision for your congregation, there will come an undeniable need for resources: people resources, financial resources, material resources and spiritual resources. When resources are needed for implementing the vision God has given you and your congregation, to whom will you turn? Where do you look for resources?

There are many possible resource providers. If we need financial resources, we might turn to a bank, a rich relative, friends, our denomination, other churches, conduct a financial campaign, or hold a rummage sale.

If you have resource needs, consider the story of Abraham, the father of faith. In the story of Abraham, found in Genesis 22, God invited Abraham to take his one and only son and sacrifice him on Mount Moriah. This was all really to test Abraham's faith. Abraham arrived at the top of Mount Moriah, built an altar and obedient to what God asked of him, laid his son on the altar.

Just as Abraham is about to bring down the knife and kill his son, a voice from heaven called out, *"Do not lay a hand on the boy. Do not do anything to him. Now I know that you fear God, because you have not withheld from me your son, your only son."* At that very moment, Abraham looked up and saw, in a near-by thicket, a ram caught by its horns. He went over and took the ram and sacrificed it as a burnt offering instead of his son.

"Abraham called that place Yahweh Yireh. And to this day it is said, "On the mountain of the LORD it will be provided." Yahweh Yireh means *"the LORD will provide." Jehoveh Yireh* is one of the names of God.

This is one of my very favorite names of God and one that, through the years, has meant the most to me. *"The Lord will provide."* God wants us to know that this His name, His nature, to provide for us.

Our God is quite capable of providing for us. In Psalm 50:10 God says, *"Every animal of the forest is mine, and the cattle on a thousand hills."* Everything belongs to God. God owns it all! His resources are without end. As you lead toward the vision God has for your congregation, never forget that God will provide. Where God guides, God will provide!

EXERCISE: Unlimited resources

If you suddenly had unlimited resources, what would you attempt for God? Think about this and write your idea down.

"If suddenly the lack of resources did not stand in the way of my vision, I would . . .

_____

_____

_____

_____

_____

_____
                                                    ”
_____—.”

EXPOSURE: How God provides

As you move toward the vision God has for you and your congregation, as you influence others toward the vision God has for your congregation, there will be a need for resources. Take time right now to read the six chapters of Exodus 13-18. You're going to find six wonderfully encouraging stories strung together, like pearls on a necklace, illustrating how God provides for those who put their trust in Him.

The story of God's provision of *guidance*. Very early in their journey toward the Promise Land, God provided Moses and the people of Israel His guidance in a most remarkable way. We read in Exodus 13:20-22: *"20 After leaving Sukkoth they camped at Etham on the edge of the desert. 21 By day the Lord went ahead of them in a pillar of cloud to guide them on their way and by night in a pillar of fire to give them light, so that they could travel by day or night. 22 Neither the pillar of cloud by day nor the pillar of fire by night left its place in front of the people."* Pretty amazing, don't you think?

God still provides guidance for our spiritual journeys today. We need guidance because, just as with Moses and the Israelites, the spiritual journey is long and challenging; and there are battles to be fought. Spiritual leaders *grasp* the importance of God's guidance as God is the Leader of leaders, the Lord of lords. Spiritual leaders know that they are only as effective as they lead people in the direction God has for the people.

Today, God still provides guidance. He doesn't guide us by a pillar of cloud by day and a pillar of fire by night. But God still guides.

- **God guides us today through His Word.** The psalmist reminds us that: *"Your word is a lamp for my feet, a light on my path."* (Psalm 119:105) Much of what God wants to accomplish in our lives and directions He want to take us are in His Word, the Bible. Effective spiritual leaders will be persons who have a good grasp of God's Word and are living it out themselves.

- **God guides us today through prayer.** Even the best leaders' knowledge and wisdom is limited. But we can ask God to provide us knowledge and wisdom. Many times, as a leader, I have not known what action or course to take, but prayer has many times brought answers. James 1:5 says, *"⁵If any of you lacks wisdom, you should ask God, who gives generously to all without finding fault, and it will be given to you."*

- **God guides us today through His Holy Spirit.** God through His Spirit provides leadings and promptings in our lives. In Acts 16:6-7 we read about one example of the leading of the Holy Spirit in the life of the great apostle Paul where God gave him direction. *"⁶Paul and his companions traveled throughout the region of Phrygia and Galatia, having been kept by the Holy Spirit from preaching the word in the province of Asia. ⁷When they came to the border of Mysia, they tried to enter Bithynia, but the Spirit of Jesus would not allow them to."* The Holy Spirit within us can provide us a strong sense of *leading*, or *urging*, or *prompting* to take a certain direction or not.

- **God guides us today through wise, godly counsel.** The most effective leaders I've known have been marked by a humility which is willing to say, *"I could be wrong."* These leaders often test their ideas with other leaders and seek wise counsel from other leaders especially when these leaders have more experience in a particular area. There is so much wisdom in the words of Proverbs 15:22 that *"Plans fail for lack of counsel, but with many* *advisers they succeed."* God has provided amazing guidance in my life through the wise and godly counsel of others.

The story of God's provision of *"a way."* What you will see, as we continue this journey with Moses and the people of Israel, is that God does not always remove the challenges in our lives, but God will provide a way through the challenges. God does not always make the way easier for us by removing a challenge we may be facing. Following Christ as a Christian does not mean that God removes all the obstacles of life.

So often our prayers are that a situation or a challenge or an obstacle be removed from our lives. Perhaps it would be better to pray, *"God make me stronger to bring me through this situation, this challenge, this obstacle."*

As we already saw in Exodus 14, God provided a way through for the Israelites when there appeared to be no way. Pharaoh, king of Egypt, pursued the Israelites and overtook them as they camped by the Red Sea. The Israelites looked up, and there were the Egyptians, marching after them. The Israelites were terrified.

One fear response is anger. The Israelites, terrified by the prospect of being slaughtered by the Egyptians in the desert, railed against Moses. But Moses calmly replied, *"Do not be afraid. Stand firm and you will see the deliverance the LORD will bring you today. The Egyptians you see today you will never see again. The LORD will fight for you; you need only to be still."*

God had Moses stretch out his hand over the sea and the waters were divided, and the Israelites went through the sea on dry ground, with a wall of water on their right and on their left. The Egyptians pursued them, and waters came back over them and they were all drowned. When the Israelites saw the great power the Lord displayed against the Egyptians, the people feared the Lord and put their trust in him and in Moses, His servant.

When you are faced with a challenge, a roadblock, or an obstacle, Henry Blackaby, in his book *Experiencing God,* invites us to look around and see where God is at work; then join God in what he is doing. When you look around to see where God is at work, you may very well see an open door. When you see that door so clearly opened before you, when you see the waters part, when you so clearly see what can only be described as a *"God moment,"* walk through it in faith and join what God has provided for you.

The story of God's provision of water. When you are in the desert, water is essential to surviving. Water is one of those essential resources you've got to have when you're in the dry, arid desert. In Exodus 15: 22-27, we read about how God provided water in the desert.

> ²² *Then Moses led Israel from the Red Sea and they went into the Desert of Shur. For three days they traveled in the desert without finding water.* ²³ *When they came to Marah, they could not drink its water because it was bitter. (That is why the place is called Marah.)* ²⁴ *So the people grumbled against Moses, saying, "What are we to drink?"* ²⁵ *Then Moses cried out to the LORD, and the LORD showed him a piece of wood. He threw it into the water, and the water became fit to drink. There the LORD issued a ruling and instruction for them and put them to the test.* ²⁶ *He said, "If you listen carefully to the LORD your God and do what is right in his eyes, if you pay attention to his commands and keep all his decrees, I will not bring on you any of the diseases I brought on the Egyptians, for I am the LORD, who heals you."* ²⁷ *Then they came to Elim, where there were twelve springs and seventy palm trees, and they camped there near the water.*

Moses led Israel from the Red Sea into the Desert of Shur. Almost immediately Moses experiences the difficulty of leaving the sea and its life-giving waters. Oftentimes, the role of the leader is to push the people away from places in which they have a tendency to remain, places of comfort, in order for them to expand their horizons and experiences and grow.

The trek through the aridity of the desert is challenging, and after traveling for three days, the people of Israel find no water. Ironically, three days before they were immersed in the waters of the Red Sea. The text does not say there was no water, but they found no water. They become disappointed, despondent and broken in spirit because of their inability to find a source of deliverance. This aridity may well point to the spiritual dryness of the people.

It is on the leadership of Moses and Miriam to show that even in the most parched desert they can find life-giving water. They finally come upon an oasis, called Marah, because its water is bitter. How great must have been their disappointment!

So how did the people respond? They grumbled against Moses, saying, *"What are we to drink?"* You are seeing a word that will be repeated many times in the book of Exodus, the word *"grumbled."* Their negative feelings get directed toward their leader, Moses. Complaints often come to the doorstep of the leader.

Every leader will hear grumbling from time to time. Do not allow grumbling or the fear that people might grumble, keep you from leading where God has invited you to lead. Leaders must have thick skins, since they frequently are the target of their followers' criticism, whether it is justified or not. It goes with the turf. Those who take on the mantle of leadership set the path that the people pursue. If things do not go according to plans and expectations, leaders should expect criticism.

Yet, it is crucial for every leader to hear the voices of the people, even if they are raised in complaint about the leader's actions. An important leadership skill that far too few value is listening. Listen to your people! Great leaders are ready to hear complaints and accept criticism in order to make things better. Moses doesn't get angry with them. It is important for every leader to be perceived as approachable, and for the leader to remain positive and focused no matter what he might be feeling—in order to move the people forward.

How did Moses respond? Moses cried out to the Lord. Crying out to the Lord in prayer is an important spiritual discipline and appropriate response for leaders. When leaders are faced with an impossible situation where we know *"we can't,"* we need to turn to the One who can. The Lord showed Moses a piece of wood which Moses threw into the water, and the water became sweet.

Here is another lesson for us about how God provides for those who put their trust in Him. Where God guides, God provides! Sometimes leaders have headed out in a direction of their own choosing without consulting God, and then, when the find themselves in the desert without water, they ask God to provide for them. Listen and write this truth down somewhere: If we move in a direction where God does not guide, we should not expect God to provide. On the other hand, we can be confident that if God guides us in a certain direction, God will provide for us.

But Moses didn't allow them to stay there. They headed out again through the desert. To lead others, a leader must be a model of action. A leader must have a bias toward taking action. Once again, as they find themselves in the desert, seemingly without any water to drink, the question is: Would they continue to trust in God's presence and God's leading to deliver them through Moses?

Unknown to the Israelites, who continued to complain that they couldn't find water to drink, not far from Marah, at Elim, there were twelve springs of fresh water and some seventy trees, and they ended up camping there. The twelve springs mentioned are interpreted as symbols of the twelve tribes of Israel, while the seventy palm trees are believed to represent the seventy elders, the leaders of the people.

So, when the people reached Elim, they had enough to eat and drink to prepare themselves for the rest of the journey. What they were going to learn was that what they lacked most was not food and water, but rather faith and courage of conviction. There was still so much God wanted to accomplish in them and there was a long way to go.

The story of God's provision of food. In Exodus 16, we read how God provided manna and quail from heaven. The whole Israelite community set out from Elim and came to the Desert of Sin, which is between Elim and Sinai. But as before, the whole community grumbled against Moses and Aaron because they were hungry. I told you *"grumbling"* is something every leader is going to hear; and so, you'll have to get used to it! Don't be surprised by it! Don't be unnerved by it!

Again, the Israelites complained, *"If only we had died by the LORD's hand in Egypt!"* God heard their complaining and provided for the Israelites bread from heaven in the morning and quail in the evening, and God said, *"Maybe then they will know that I am the LORD their God."*

Now most people think the word manna means *"bread."* In fact, the word *"manna"* literally means *"What is it?"* They were saying to each other, *"What the heck is this?"* They hadn't seen anything like this before. But God provided this *"What is it?"* every day. It was delivered fresh—not stale—but fresh every day; just as the Bible says that God's mercies are fresh and new every day. They could not hoard the bread. The day-old bread got stale quickly.

Here is another important truth about God's provision: God gives us our daily bread, so that we come to trust Him! God wants us looking to Him as our Provider. God wants to build our faith in Him to provide. God provided *"daily bread"* so that the people of Israel, as well as you and me, would look to Him every day for the day's provision.

This is why Jesus, in the Lord's Prayer, gave us this petition, *"Give us today our daily bread."* (Matthew 6:11) In this prayer we're saying to God, *"Lord, I am turning to You as my Provider of my daily needs, understanding that I'll need to come to You tomorrow for tomorrow's daily bread."* God will provide, but daily, so that you and I come to put our complete trust in Him.

The *story* of God's provision of water from a rock. In Exodus 17:1-7, we read how God provided water from the rock. This is the second water story. You can never get enough water in the desert.

Once again in their journey through the desert, there was no water for the people to drink. And once again the people of Israel grumbled:

> *"Give us water to drink." Moses replied, "Why do you quarrel with me? Why do you put the Lord to the test?" 3 But the people were thirsty for water there, and they grumbled against Moses. They said, "Why did you bring us up out of Egypt to make us and our children and livestock die of thirst?"4 Then Moses cried out to the Lord, "What am I to do with these people? They are almost ready to stone me." 5 The Lord answered Moses, "Go out in front of the people. Take with you some of the elders of Israel and take in your hand the staff with which you struck the Nile, and go. 6 I will stand there before you by the rock at Horeb. Strike the rock, and water will come out of it for the people to drink." So Moses did this in the sight of the elders of Israel. 7 And he called the place Massah and Meribah because the Israelites quarreled and because they tested the Lord saying, "Is the Lord among us or not?"*

Moses' frustration with the people began to show. He cried out to the Lord, *"What am I to do with these people?"* For a leader, it takes strength of character and a commitment to the long-term vision to be able to listen to people, especially when they voice strong criticism or objection to your leadership. It is difficult not to take it personally and not respond in a defensive and angry way.

Moses may have wanted to walk away from *"these people"* but God directs him *"go out in front"* or *"pass by the people."* Leaders must overcome the impulse to withdraw and isolate themselves, especially from those who challenge our leadership. Every leader must work hard to stay connected to the people he or she is leading.

Leaders must get out among their people, to listen and learn from them. Do not withdraw and hold a grudge. *"Pass by"* or *"go out among"* the people to connect with them. Interestingly, the verb *"pass"* can also mean *"forgive."* So, God could have been inviting Moses to walk among the people and forgive them. God also commanded, that when he passed before the people, to bring along with him some of the elders of Israel. Moses was urged to take advantage of the support of the other leaders of the community.

Then God directed Moses, *"I will stand there before you by the rock at Horeb. Strike the rock, and water will come out of it for the people to drink."* So Moses did this in the sight of the elders of Israel and water gushed forth.

There is something else to be considered in the return to Horeb and the rock. God is often referred to as "The Rock" in the Bible, and so in directing Moses and the people to Horeb and the rock, God is pointing them to the source of life-giving water for all of us—Himself.

In 1 Corinthians 10:1-4 we read a New Testament reference to this story. *"For I do not want you to be ignorant of the fact, brothers, that our forefathers were all under the cloud and that they all passed through the sea. They were all baptized into Moses in the cloud and in the sea. They all ate the same spiritual food and drank the same spiritual drink; for they drank from the spiritual rock that accompanied them, and that rock was Christ."*

That rock was Christ! Isn't this an incredible thought?

The people of Israel doubted God being with them. Moses called the place Massah and Meribah because the Israelites quarreled and because they tested the Lord saying, *"Is the LORD among us or not?"* The Israelites doubted. They could not, would not, believe that the Lord was with them. But Christ was with them in the desert, every step of the way. Jesus was the Rock who accompanied them.

The principle about God's provision that we need to see here in this story is that our most important resource in the spiritual journey is our relationship with Christ! In Christ, our parched spiritual souls get refreshed for the long journey from our Egypt to our Promise Land. Christ is with us in the journey, refreshing us and strengthening us for the journey, and accompanying us in the journey!

The story of God's provision of people to help. In Exodus 18, we find Moses leading the people, trying to shepherd them all by himself. One day, Moses' father-in-law, Jethro comes alongside Moses and says, *"What you are doing is not good. You and these people who come to you will only wear yourselves out. The work is too heavy for you; you cannot handle it alone."* Jethro's concern was that Moses would tire himself out.

So, Jethro goes on to counsel Moses to *"Select capable men from all the people—men who fear God, trustworthy men who hate dishonest gain—and appoint them as officials over thousands, hundreds, fifties and tens. Have them serve as judges for the people at all times, but have them bring every difficult case to you; the simple cases they can decide themselves."*

One of the most overlooked resources in our journey toward God's vision for our congregations is the people God brings into our lives. God's provision sometimes comes in the form of people. Sometimes the needs and challenges we face can be addressed by the people God has brought around us.

It was flooding in California. As the flood waters were rising, a man was on the stoop of his house and another man in a rowboat came by. The man in the rowboat told the man on the stoop to get in and he'd save him. The man on the stoop said, *"No!"* He had faith in God and would wait for God to save him. The flood waters kept rising and the man had to go to the second floor of his house.

A man in a motorboat came by and told the man in the house to get in because he had come to rescue him. The man in the house said, *"No thank you!"* He had perfect faith in God and would wait for God to save him. The flood waters kept rising.

Pretty soon the water was up to the man's roof and he got out on the roof. A helicopter then came by, lowered a rope and the pilot shouted down to the man in the house to climb up the rope because the helicopter had come to rescue him. The man in the house wouldn't get in. He told the pilot that he had faith in God and would wait for God to rescue him. The flood waters kept rising and the man in the house drowned.

When this man got to heaven, he asked God where he went wrong. He told God that he had perfect faith in Him, but wondered why God had let him drown. *"What more do you want from me?"* asked God. *"For crying out loud, I sent you two boats and a lifeguard. What more did you want?"*

Sometimes we look for God's provision in every place except right around us, with the people God has brought into our lives. Every effective leader understands that people are an incredible resource, perhaps one of the most important resources. People are the most important resource a leader has!

Now, there is a recurring pattern in all these stories. Did you see it? The people *"grumbled"* while God faithfully provided. Grumbling, in all these stories, is an expression of faithlessness. The people refused to accept that God was with them and that God would provide for them.

If you work with people, if you lead people, you will experience grumbling. I believe that Exodus 16:8 will help you keep grumbling in perspective. *"Moses said, 'You will know that it was the LORD when he gives you meat to eat in the evening and all the bread you want in the morning, because he has heard your grumbling against him. Who are we? You are not grumbling against us, but against the LORD.'"*

When you are leading in the direction God has invited you to lead, grumbling will feel like a personal attack. Try your best not to take it personally. Like Moses, keep in mind that grumbling is an expression of faithlessness and that it is really directed toward the Lord, and that God will ultimately deal with this.

EXERCISE: *Your story of God's provision*

Which of the five stories of God's providing for the Israelites, is closest to a story of how God has personally provided for you? Tell your story:

_____

_____

_____

_____

_____

_____

_____

EXPOSURE: *Your need for resources*

Many of us, because of our lack of faith and vision, operate with what I call a *"scarcity mindset."* Because of our lack of faith and perspective we imagine that we don't have enough: enough money, enough people, or enough equipment to accomplish what God has called us to do.

Only when we grasp the truth that God owns everything so that there is no lack of resources with God, and that God wants to be our Provider, will we begin operating with what I call an *"abundance mindset."* With an abundance mindset, a leader can operate with great confidence that where God guides, God will provide. There is no question in the mind of such a leader that God won't provide. The only remaining questions for such a leader is *When?* and *How?*

The Apostle Paul, in speaking to the Christians in Philippi, wrote: *"My God will meet all your needs according to his glorious riches in Christ Jesus."* (Philippians 4:19) Notice that I underlined the word, *"all"* as in *"all your needs."* I didn't want you to miss the truth that there is not a need that God cannot meet.

Now, let's be clear that God promises to meet our need, just not our greed! We all have needs and we all have wants. Our wants can be a reflection of our greed. But we can operate with a great degree of confidence that God will provide for all the needs as we move toward the vision God has for our congregation.

A LEADER'S KEY RESOURCES

- **Spiritual resources.** In the journey toward God's vision for your congregation, there will be spiritual needs. The leader and the congregation will have need for wisdom, patience, strength, understanding, grace, discernment and the list could go on.

Now, one of the observations you should have made in reading Exodus, chapters 13-18, is that God did not always remove the challenges for Moses and the Israelites. Rather than removing all our challenges, God will often provide spiritual resources to bring us through the challenges.

For instance, on three occasions the Apostle Paul pleaded with God to remove a burden in his own life, but God's provision was not to remove the burden, but to provide the spiritual resource of grace. Paul writes that God's answer to his prayer was: *"My grace is sufficient for you, for my power is made perfect in weakness."* (2 Corinthians 12:9) God has an abundance of spiritual resources to meet all our spiritual needs!

- **Material resources.** In the journey toward God's vision for your congregation, there will also be material needs which include financial needs, facility needs, curriculum needs, computer needs, transportation needs, and staffing needs, just to name a few. God knows the needs we have before we ever become conscious of them, and God has promised to provide for our needs.

When we become aware of our needs, God invites us to come to Him and ask Him to meet those needs as our Provider. We do need to do a better job, distinguishing between our need and our greed. But James 4:2 says, *"You want something, but don't get it. You kill and covet, but you cannot have what you want. You quarrel and fight. You do not have, because you do not ask God."* We often go without, because we have gone without praying! Great spiritual leaders are men and women, who recognize their absolute dependence upon God, pray fervently and continuously that God would meet their needs.

- **People resources.** In the journey toward God's vision for your congregation, there will undoubtedly be people needs. I often hear a leader say, *"I need more leaders"* or *"I need more people to accomplish this ministry."* God knows our need for people resources, and sometimes God will bring a person to our congregation who is the perfect fit for the need we have.

However, one of the most over-looked resources in this area are the people that God already has surrounding us. Sometimes, the leader we need or the people we feel we need to accomplish the ministry, are right in front of our noses. We just haven't asked them, or we haven't taken time to develop them.

Take some time to think about some of the people in your congregation with the gifts and passions God has given to them. If you asked them and they were willing, if you put a little time into training them and developing them, might they be the answer to your people need?

EXERCISE: All your needs

Philippians 4:6 says: *"Do not be anxious about anything, but in everything, by prayer and petition, with thanksgiving, present your requests to God."* Present your requests to God. In this exercise, take time to think and pray. Think about, anticipate all the needs you will have as you lead into the future. Write down these needs and spend time asking God to provide for you.

A LEADER'S KEY RESOURCES

Spiritual needs _____ _____ _____

_____ _____ _____

_____ _____ _____

_____ _____ _____

_____ _____ _____

Material needs _____ _____ _____

_____ _____ _____

_____ _____ _____

_____ _____ _____

_____ _____ _____

People needs _____ _____ _____

_____ _____ _____

_____ _____ _____

_____ _____ _____

_____ _____ _____

EXPERIENCE: Praying leaders

Hear this again: *We often go without, because we have gone without praying!* In groups of three or four, have each person share their top three prayer requests and then have the group pray for the needs and for God to provide.

CHAPTER 10

THE LEADERSHIP
SKILL OF DELEGATING

Exodus 17 & 18

KEY PRINCIPLE: ONE OF THE MOST EFFECTIVE, YET MOST NEGLECTED, SKILLS IN LEADERSHIP IS DELEGATING!

"I believe that a leader's success can be defined as the maximum utilization of the abilities of those under him."
—John Maxwell

EXPOSURE: Why do we try to do it alone?

A brick layer, trying to do it by himself, wrote the following letter to an insurance company to explain his injuries:

Dear Sir: I am writing in response to your request for more information concerning block No. 11 on the insurance form, which asks for *"Cause of injuries,"* wherein I put *"trying to do the job alone."* You said you needed more information, so I trust the following will be sufficient: I am a bricklayer by trade, and on the date of injuries I was working alone laying bricks around the top of a four-story building, when suddenly I realized that I had about 500 pounds of bricks left over. Rather than carry the bricks down by hand, I decided to put them into a barrel and lower them by a pulley that was fastened to the top of the building. I secured the end of the rope at ground level and went up to the top of the building, loaded the brick into the barrel, and flung the barrel out with the bricks in it. I then went down and untied the rope, holding it securely to insure the slow descent of the barrel.

As you will note in block No. 6 of the insurance form, I weigh 145 pounds. Due to my shock at being jerked off the ground so swiftly, I lost my presence of mind and forgot to let go of the rope. Between the second and third floors I met the barrel, coming down. This accounts for the bruises and lacerations on my upper body. Upon regaining my presence of mind, I held tightly to the rope and proceeded rapidly up the side of the building, not stopping until my right hand was jammed into the pulley. This accounts for my broken thumb. Despite the pain, I retained my presence of mind and held tightly to the rope. At approximately the same time, however, the barrel of bricks hit the ground and the bottom fell out of the barrel. Devoid of the weight of the bricks, the barrel now weighed about 50 pounds. I again refer you to block No. 6 and my weight. As you would guess, I began a rapid descent. In the vicinity of the second floor, I met the empty barrel coming up. This explains the injuries to my legs and lower body. Slowed only slightly, I continued my descent, landing on the pile of bricks. Fortunately, my back was only sprained, and the internal injuries were minimal. I am sorry to report, however, that at this point I again lost my presence of mind and let go of the rope. As you can imagine, the empty barrel crashed down on top of me. I trust that this answers your concern. Please know that I am finished *"trying to do the job alone."*

Yours sincerely,

The bricklayer in the story discovered, the hard way, what a lot of us find out sooner or later in life: trying to do the job or trying to do life alone can be a hazardous enterprise. Nevertheless, rugged individualism is prized and valued in many cultures. God, on the other hand, values relationships and community.

Why do we tend to want to do things by ourselves and not ask for help? Consider that we all start out in life in **dependent** relationships. When we were first born, we were all dependent upon our parents.

Our parents provided us with food, clothing, and shelter. Dependence means this:

- Needing and relying on others for life needs
- Being unable or unwilling to provide for one's self
- Relying upon the aid of others

As we get older, we move away from dependence to becoming **independent**. A realization comes that we are not like everyone else. We want to be independent. So, we assert our attitudes and behaviors believing that if we are free from others, we will be independent. Culturally, we equate maturity and mature relationships with independence. We value and we celebrate when our children discover, *"I can do it all by myself."*

Independence means this:

- Not needing or relying upon others for life or relational needs
- Being able to provide for one's self
- Free from the influence, guidance and control of others

However, God calls us not to be dependent or independent, but to be **interdependent** and to have interdependent relationships. Interdependent means this:

- Committing who we are and what we have to serve together
- Knowing what we can offer to others, and what we need from others
- Enjoying life in mutually beneficial relationships

God never intended us to *"do life"* alone. This is why God gave us family, marriage, friends, community, and the church. We can see God's design for interdependence within the church through a metaphor given to us in Romans 12 and 1 Corinthians 12, where the church is described like a human body with its many parts and with all the parts working together.

EXERCISE: *You are the body of Christ and each one of you is a part of it!*

Take some time to read about the metaphor of the church as the body of Christ and visualize what that would be like. Read Romans 12:3-8 and the entirety of 1 Corinthians 12, and identify at least five lessons or principles for how the church is to operate.

1. _____

_____

_____

_____

2. _____

_____

_____

_____

3. _____

_____

_____

_____

4. _____

_____

_____

_____

5. _____

_____

_____

_____

6. _____

_____

_____

_____

In a single word, the word picture I want you to begin entertaining in your mind as you pursue God's vision for your life and the life of your congregation is that we operate as a *"TEAM."* Begin thinking of your congregation as the team God has invited you to play on and serve as coach. As one of the leaders on the team, I want to encourage you to think of yourself as a player coach. What is a player coach, and what is he or she supposed to do?

I think we are given an understanding of spiritual leaders as player coaches in Ephesians 4:11-13 where it says that *"[11] Christ himself gave the apostles, the prophets, the evangelists, the pastors and teachers, [12] to equip his people for works of service, so that the body of Christ may be built up [13] until we all reach unity in the faith and in the knowledge of the Son of God and become mature, attaining to the whole measure of the fullness of Christ."*

Spiritual leaders are not to do all the work of ministry. Spiritual leaders are to equip the people for the work of ministry so that the body of Christ may be built up. This requires developing people and delegating ministry assignments to others so that the church operates most effectively.

EXPOSURE: Every leader needs support

While God imparted His vision for the Israelites to Moses, God never meant for the vision to be Moses' alone or for Moses to implement the vision all by himself. Mind you, Moses started leading thinking, like a lot of leaders, of himself as a *"lone ranger."*

But again, and again, God pointed Moses to others who would serve alongside him like Aaron, the elders and Miriam. Breaking the pattern of thinking of oneself as a *"lone leader,"* is not an easy pattern to break. Like all leaders, Moses was learning and developing as a leader.

We pick up the story in Exodus 17:8. Immediately after God had provided water, *"the Amalekites came and attacked the Israelites at Rephidim."* Note that Moses did not lead the Israelites into battle. He is gradually learning that he can't do everything. What Moses did is he delegated to Joshua, the son of Nun, to choose men to fight the Amalekites. *"Moses said to Joshua, 'Choose some of our men and go out to fight the Amalekites. Tomorrow I will stand on top of the hill with the staff of God in my hands.'"* (Exodus 17:9)

One of the skills that continued to be developed in Moses' life, over a long period of time, was the skill of delegation—where he grew in his willingness to share the burden of leading people. In delegating leadership to Joshua, Moses empowered Joshua to lead the Israelites into battle. A leader must learn how to recognize the talents of his or her followers and place the right people in the right positions to get the job done. This is a key to effective leadership. It's called delegation.

Delegating to others and helping them develop leadership character, skills and ability is the responsibility of every good leader. John Maxwell writes: *"I believe that a leader's success can be defined as the maximum utilization of the abilities of those under him."*

Developing future leaders is one of the most important legacies of a leader—those whom the leader has developed and delegated ministry. It comes with the recognition that the leader cannot lead alone. Like all leaders, Moses is learning that he has no choice, if Israel is to realize God's vision, but to involve others in various leadership and support roles.

Delegation, however, is not abdication of leadership. Great leaders delegate: but leaders don't delegate aspects of leading for which they alone are responsible. Though Moses commanded Joshua to lead the Israelites into battle, Moses himself continued to be the vehicle through which God's presence inspired the Israelites to battle and defeat the Amalekites.

At the outset of the battle, Moses positioned himself on top of the nearest hill with the rod of God in his hand. Moses held the rod above his head, as the rod represented a kind of battle flag, from which soldiers in battle drew strength. *"As long as Moses held up his hands, the Israelites were winning, but whenever he lowered his hands, the Amalekites were winning. When Moses' hands grew tired, they took a stone and put it under him and he sat on it. Aaron and Hur held his hands up—one on one side, one on the other—so that his hands remained steady till sunset."* (Exodus 17:11-12)

In raising his hands towards the heavens, Moses was reminding the people of the One who appointed Moses as leader, to the One who had been their ultimate Leader and the One who had always been the source of their strength and redemption. With hands pointing to the real power, Moses can be seen as praying to God for protection and victory.

As long as Moses held up his hands, the Israelites were winning, but whenever he lowered his hands, the Amalekites were winning. The actions of the leader have impact on the destiny of the people he or she leads. But the opposite is true as well. People can have an impact on their leaders, as we are about to see.

As the battle continued, Moses' hands became heavy, weighed down by the burden of leadership. Moses' brother, Aaron, and his nephew, Hur, saw what was happening and so *"they took a stone and put it under and he sat on it. Aaron and Hur held his hands up—one on one side, one on the other—so that his hands remained steady till sunset. So Joshua overcame the Amalekite army with the sword."* (Exodus 17:12-13)

The point being made seems to be that, through the effort of Aaron and Hur, Moses' faith was bolstered, even in the face of the enemy. Moses, like every leader, needed support. People, through their actions, can bolster the courage of their leaders. The truth is all leaders need support to face and overcome the challenges common to leading.

Aaron and Hur placed a rock under Moses so he could sit down. One can't help but associate God with the rock, since God is usually referred to as *"The Rock"* in the Bible, and Moses' greatest support comes from God.

"When traditional commentators ask why Aaron and Hur place a hard, uncomfortable stone under Moses, they usually emphasize that he refuses to sit on anything else because he wants to identify with his people." (Norman J. Cohen, *Moses and the Journey to Leadership*, p 85) Moses didn't want a place too comfortable while his men were battling. Effective leaders do not separate themselves from the people they lead. They put themselves "in the trenches" with their people.

Upon the victory over the Amalekites, "the Lord said to Moses, 'Write this on a scroll as something to be remembered and make sure that Joshua hears it, because I will completely blot out the name of Amalek from under heaven.' Moses built an altar and called it The Lord is my Banner. He said, 'Because hands were lifted up against the throne of the Lord, the Lord will be at war against the Amalekites from generation to generation.'" (Exodus 17:14-16)

EXERCISE: Why do some leaders fail to delegate?

Below is a list of reasons why some leaders fail to delegate or share ministry. The list is not complete. There is room for you to add some other reasons. Check which reasons cause you to not delegate.

- Insecurity _____
- Habit of doing ministry yourself _____

- "I can do it better." _____
- "It's just easier to do it myself." _____
- Lack of time _____
- Reluctance due to past failures _____
- Lack of confidence in others _____
- Personal enjoyment of doing the task _____
- Inability to find someone to do it _____
- "I don't know how to delegate." _____
- _____
- _____

EXPOSURE: *The Jethro Principle*

Delegation is one of the most powerful tools of a leader. It is a learned skill, a skill that requires lots of practice. It is so easy to slip back into being a "lone ranger" leader and doing everything yourself as we are about to see in Exodus 18:14. *"When his father-in-law saw all that Moses was doing for the people, he said, 'What is this you are doing for the people? Why do you alone sit as judge, while all these people stand around you from morning till evening?'"*

What we are about to see is that God used Moses' father-in-law, Jethro to speak some good, Godly counsel into Moses' life. Moses was God's appointed leader of the Israelites. But God used Moses' father-in-law Jethro to coach Moses on an important aspect of leadership that we are focusing on in this chapter.

Notice Jethro's excellent coaching style. Jethro first spent some time observing Moses. What does Jethro see? Moses' father-in-law, who just arrived in the Israelite camp, observed the heavy responsibilities that Moses is carrying. He sees that Moses is behaving like a king over his subjects.

It was only after he spent time observing Moses, that Jethro asked Moses some questions. *"The next day Moses took his seat to serve as judge for the people, and they stood around him from morning till evening. When his father-in-law saw all that Moses was doing for the people, he said, 'What is this you are doing for the people? Why do you alone sit as judge, while all these people stand around you from morning till evening?'"* (Exodus 18: 13-14)

Good coaching involves good questions. Jethro asked two great questions: What are you doing? And, why are you doing what you are doing?" These are two questions that every leader should ask of himself or herself from time to time. What am I doing? Why am I doing this?

Moses was convinced that only he could play all the major roles, as he explains: *"Because the people come to me to seek God's will. Whenever they have a dispute, it is brought to me, and I decide between the parties and inform them of God's decrees and laws."* (Exodus 18:15-16) Moses clearly thought he was doing a good thing, even a Godly thing, by helping the people with disputes about God's decrees and laws. But perhaps Moses' ego had gotten in the way causing him to think that only he could handle the cases. Leaders must be willing to acknowledge that they can't control and run everything. This requires humility.

Jethro replied, *"17 What you are doing is not good. 18 You and these people who come to you will only wear yourselves out' The work is too heavy for you; you cannot handle it alone."* (Exodus 18:17-18) Note how Jethro's critique on Moses' leadership style is done with great sensitivity and grace, so that Moses can hear his advice without becoming defensive. He did not tell Moses that what he was doing was bad or evil, but chose to phrase it as *"not good."*

What could possibly be *"not good"* about what Moses was doing? Moses was probably thinking, *"All I am trying to do is meet the needs of the people who come to me!"* Note that Jethro took the time to show Moses the impact that his actions are having on the people and on himself.

We can learn something here from Jethro about coaching a developing leader. It's as if Jethro is raising the question to Moses, *"Do you imagine that there could be a better way of accomplishing your goal?"* By the way, this is another good coaching question you might ask yourself from time to time. Is there any better way for me to accomplish my goal?

Jethro saw the problem as three-fold:

- Jethro cautioned Moses, *"Moses, you cannot possibly handle all the needs.* "Because of Moses' diverse responsibilities and the enormity of the task of judging cases brought to him by the entire nation, the people could not gain access to Moses when they needed him though he sat in judgement of the people's cases from morning until night. *"How in the world Moses do you imagine doing it all?"*

Leaders do not have unlimited capacity to lead. As human beings— we are not God—our capacity to lead and shepherd is limited. As our congregation and surrounding community grow, so too will the needs. These needs will eventually be too great for any one leader to handle.

- Jethro cautioned Moses, *"Moses, you will wear yourself out."* In America today, fifteen hundred pastors leave the ministry each month due to moral failure, spiritual burnout or contention in their churches. 90% of the pastors report working between 55 to 75 hours per week. 80% of pastors in America believe pastoral ministry has negatively affected their families. Many pastor's children do not attend church now because of what the church has done to their parents. The possibility of burnout is a very real issue for spiritual leaders.

- Jethro cautioned Moses, *"Moses, the people will wear out too."* How would the people wear out? Well, Jethro had observed and commented, "All these people stand around you from morning till evening.'" It is wearying and frustrating to stand in line waiting to see your pastor. What wears is people's patience with the pastor. People's patience wears thin.

Moses was leading the people like a *"lone leader."* A few years ago, I read James Belasco's and Ralph Stayer's book *Flight of the Buffalo* which illustrates how many organizations—and it's true for churches—function like a herd of buffalos.

The American buffalo, more accurately called *bison* today, once roamed North America in vast herds. It is estimated that at one time there were 50 million buffalos who roamed the prairies of the American west. These would travel in herds and were absolutely loyal followers of the lead buffalo. They would do whatever the lead buffalo wanted them to do. But by 1899, there were only 835 buffalo left in the United States.

But today buffalo are almost extinct. Organized groups of hunters killed buffalo for hides and meat, often killing up to 250 buffalo a day. Entire herds were wiped out as the early settlers realized that when they shot the lead buffalo, the herd stood there, waiting for their leader to lead them, while the hunters picked them off one at a time.

Using the metaphor of how a buffalo leads, Belasco and Stayer relate how many organizations operate by one leader, one voice, a central command, high level control, and a clear hierarchy. Their book offers step-by-step advice on how to lead from a herd of dependent, standing-around-waiting-for-instructions buffalo to a flock of inter-dependent, leadership sharing geese—all focused on serving customers.

The flight of geese is another and contrasting metaphor. Consider the following lessons from the geese. You can view this part of the lesson through a YouTube video called A Lesson from Geese on your computer. Go to   https://youtu.be/dXL5M30A_sg_ [English] Go to   https://youtu.be/K5G8gRvx7nQ   [Spanish]

- **Fact:** As each goose flaps its wings, it creates "uplift" for the birds that follow. By flying in a "V" formation, the whole flock adds 71% greater flying range than if each bird flies alone.

Lesson: People who share a common direction and sense of community can get where they are going quicker and easier, because they are travelling on the thrust of one another.

- **Fact:** When a goose falls out of formation, it suddenly feels the drag and resistance of flying alone. It then quickly moves back into formation to take advantage of the lifting power of the bird immediately in front of it.

  Lesson: If we have as much sense as a goose, we will stay in formation with those headed where we want to go. We will be willing to accept their help and give our help to others.

- **Fact:** When the lead goose tires, it rotates back into the formation and another goose flies to the point position.

  Lesson: It pays to take turns doing the hard tasks and sharing leadership. As with geese, people are interdependent on each other's skills, capabilities and unique arrangement of gifts, talents and resources.

- **Fact:** The geese flying in formation honk to encourage those up front to keep up their speed.

  Lesson: We need to make sure our *"honking"* is encouraging. In groups where there is encouragement, the production is much greater. The power of encouragement (to stand by one's heart and core values and encourage the heart and core values of others) is the quality of *"honking"* we seek.

- **Fact:** When a goose gets sick, wounded or shot down, two geese drop out of formation and follow it down to help and protect it. They stay with it until it dies or is able to fly again. Then they launch out with another formation or catch up with the flock.

  Lesson: If we have as much sense as geese, we will stand by each other in difficult times as well as when we are strong.

For several years in ministry, I operated in the buffalo metaphor. I believed my job was to shepherd all the congregation, plan, organize, command, coordinate, and control. In my congregation, I was the lead buffalo. Members were loyal, but I discovered that just like a buffalo herd, a lot of members were standing around and waiting for the leader to show them what to do. When I wasn't around, they'd wait for me to show up. I saw a lot of *"waiting around"* in my buffalo-like congregation. Worse, people did only what I told them to do, nothing more, as they *"waited around"* for my next set of instructions.

I also found it was hard work being the lead buffalo. Giving all the orders, doing all the *"important"* work took 12-14 hours a day. It's exhausting being a lead buffalo! Meanwhile my congregation was getting slaughtered out there in the world because I hadn't prepared them to partner in ministry.

After a few years, I finally got it. What I really wanted in our congregation was a group of responsible, interdependent workers, like a flock of geese. I could see the geese flying in their "V" formation, the leadership changing frequently, with different geese taking the lead. I saw every goose being responsible for getting itself to wherever the gaggle was going, changing roles whenever necessary, alternating as a leader, a follower, or a scout. When the task changed, the geese would be responsible for changing the structure of the group to accommodate, similar to the geese that fly in a "V." I could see each goose being a leader.

What I came to realize was that the biggest obstacle to success was how I operated as a leader. I had to rid myself of this picture of a loyal herd of buffalo waiting for me, the leader, to tell them what to do. I knew I had to change the picture to become a different kind of leader, so everyone could function at their highest level.

Let's go back to Jethro's coaching of Moses. Jethro's coaching advice to Moses included these words of Exodus 18:19-23. Having explained what he had observed and his concerns, Jethro went on to say:

> *"¹⁹Listen now to me and I will give you some advice, and may God be with you. You must be the people's representative before God and bring their disputes to him. ²⁰ Teach them the decrees and laws, and show them the way to live and the duties they are to perform. ²¹ But select capable men from all the people—men who fear God, trustworthy men who hate dishonest gain—and appoint them as officials over thousands, hundreds, fifties and tens. ²² Have them serve as judges for the people at all times, but have them bring every difficult case to you; the simple cases they can decide themselves. That will make your load lighter, because they will share it with you. ²³ If you do this and God so commands, you will be able to stand the strain, and all these people will go home satisfied."*

Jethro's coaching points were these:

- **Be the people's representative before God.** Jethro told Moses, *"You have a role. You represent the people before God. Don't delegate the role that you alone can play."* But Moses was not to forget that these are God's people and that God is the One they are ultimately to be seeking counsel from.

But God appoints leaders for His church. If you are a leader, if you are a pastor, you need to take to heart the Apostle Paul's counsel, of Romans 12:8, where his charge to those with the gift of leadership is to *"lead with all diligence!"* We lead spiritually and diligently when we serve as God's representative among God's people.

- **Teach the people God's ways and how they are to live.** Moses was invited to teach and train the people to know God's ways so that they wouldn't get into trouble. An important aspect of being a coach is teaching and training. An effective leader-coach knows when he or she has done an adequate job of teaching and training when people know how to apply what they've been taught and not be dependent upon the leader.

- **Select capable others to help.** Moses was coached by Jethro to select capable assistant coaches to help him lead the team. Selection of *"capable"* persons is critical. Delegation isn't just putting anyone in a ministry position; it's putting the right person in the right position. Jethro even provides some basic qualifications for those Moses would end up selecting. They would be *"men who fear God, trustworthy men who hate dishonest gain."* Begin to think through the qualifications needed for a particular assignment <u>before</u> selection.

As the leader of God's congregation, begin to think of yourself as a leader of leaders. Are there some ministry responsibilities that you can delegate to other leaders, not only for the reason of sharing the load, but also to develop other leaders? Think about some of those responsibilities you can delegate and the qualifications needed, and begin to write them down.

As you begin delegating, you may find that your apprentice or developing leader will need some training and development. John Maxwell, in his book, *The 21 Irrefutable Laws of Leadership,* writes: *"Every effective leadership mentor makes the development of leaders one of his highest priorities in life."* (p.139) While you might be hesitant, thinking that it will require too much time, in the long run your investment in these leaders will help build and strengthen the team and lighten your load.

- **Break down the challenge into manageable parts and place people where they are gifted.** In Moses' case, there were:

  - Leaders over thousands
  - Leaders over hundreds
  - Leaders over fifties
  - Leaders over ten

One of the ways a leader can involve more people in ministry and in leadership is by breaking down ministry assignments into manageable parts. Once you've broken down ministry assignments into manageable parts, help people, depending on their gifts and passion, to find where they would like to serve on the team.

Notice that there are different levels of leadership requiring different abilities and skillsets by the leader. In the Bible passage you read earlier, in Romans 12 and 1 Corinthians 12, you learned about how God has designed His church so that every member has spiritual gifts or spiritual abilities and can contribute to the mission of the church.

Recognize that individuals will play different kinds of roles because not every potential leader is equipped to fulfill every role. Choices must be made based on the individual's skills, talents and leadership capabilities. Moses learned that there are indeed different levels of leadership and each person can play a role for which he or she is uniquely suited.

Delegating to others and empowering others should be a part of the playbook of every leader. All too often, leaders fail to realize the importance of sharing power and delegating authority to others. They don't understand that by empowering others, they themselves will gain. Counterintuitively, leaders who empower others increase their own power and standing among the people.

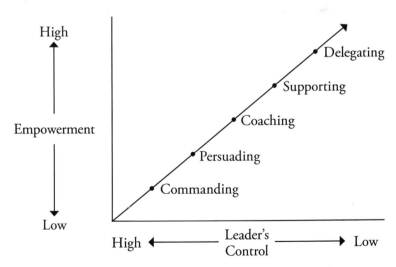

Delegating or sharing responsibility means delegating or sharing authority as well. Nothing can be more frustrating than having great responsibility without much authority. The level of authority you share should be equal to the level of responsibility you have entrusted to someone.

- **If there are more difficult issues, they can pass them along to the leader.** Some ministry assignments, perhaps many, can be delegated. However, there are some ministry assignments and some decisions that leaders cannot, nor should they, delegate. This is where leaders must be most prayerful, praying for wisdom and discernment. James 1:5 says, *"If any of you lacks wisdom, he should ask God, who gives generously to all without finding fault, and it will be given to him."*

For instance, providing the overall leadership of the team is too critical for you to delegate. In 1997, one of the finest business leaders in the world died. His name was Roberto Goizueta, and he was the chairman and chief executive of the Coca-Cola Company.

Born in Cuba and educated at Yale, where he earned a degree in chemical engineering, Roberto Goizueta, took over the leadership of Coca-Cola in 1981. The company's value at the time was $4 billion. Under Goizueta's leadership it rose to $150 billion, an increase in value of 3,500 percent!

What Roberto Goizueta was most effective doing was developing other leaders, including his successor Douglas Ivestor. But Roberto Goizueta said this: *"Leadership is one of the things you cannot delegate. You either exercise it, or you abdicate it."*

As in the case of Moses, the more difficult issues and assignments of leadership must remain the focus of the leader. You cannot delegate everything.

Let me point out one final observation about Moses. What was Moses' response to Jethro's coaching advice? Here is what we are told: *"Moses listened to his father-in-law and did everything he said. He chose capable men from all Israel and made them leaders of the people, officials over thousands, hundreds, fifties and tens. They served as judges for the people at all times. The difficult cases they brought to Moses, but the simple ones they decided themselves."* (Exodus 18:24-26)

Moses heard Jethro's coaching and he followed through on it. All great leaders open themselves to being coached. They are always open to learning. The best leaders consider themselves life-long learning leaders.

Moses was a tremendous leader, in large part, because he followed Godly counsel about delegation. When you receive good, Godly counsel, follow it!

EXERCISE: Delegating ministry and developing leaders

The instruction from Jethro provides timeless leadership principles any leader would be wise to apply. Interestingly, there is a similar story and instruction in the New Testament in Acts 6:1-7. In this well-known passage, the early church was growing rapidly, and with corresponding growing needs, to the point that some needs were not being met. Read Acts 6:1-7 and write out the transferable delegating principles for your leadership.

1. _____

_____

_____

_____

_____

2. _____
   _____
   _____
   _____
   _____

3. _____
   _____
   _____
   _____
   _____

4. _____
   _____
   _____
   _____
   _____

EXPOSURE: Spelling TEAM

No doubt, you have all heard how "Team" is spelled. Team is spelled **T.E.A.M.** which stands for *"Together Everyone Achieves More!"* We can accomplish more together than we can alone. So, let me spell it out!

T **ogether**—bound together by a common purpose, a common vision.

To be a team, you've got to have a common purpose. Legendary basketball coach John Wooden always stressed that *"a team is a group of people working together for a common purpose."*

A group of people who do not know their common purpose is not a team-even though they may call themselves a team. You can have a crowd, and not a team! A lot of churches have a crowd, but they do not operate as a team because they lack a common purpose, a common vision. And it's not just having a purpose statement on a banner, it is when every member of the team has embraced the purpose and is working towards the goal, the vision.

E **veryone**—finding their position using their unique gifts.

To be a team, everyone has a place. Real teams provide everyone a position. In the local church there is a position for everyone. Are you, as the coach of the team, playing your position and are you helping others in your congregation find their place? When people begin to find their position on the team, they will begin to find reason to play their hearts out.

A **chieves**—contributing to the mission.

God created us to be contributors, not consumers. This is the reason why *"It is more blessed to give than to receive."* (Acts 20:35) We will never find our greatest fulfillment until we are contributing. On a team where everyone has a position, where everyone is using their unique gifts, everyone experiences the satisfaction of achieving, contributing to the mission.

M **ore**—impact!

This is so true! So much more can be accomplished when we work together as a team, than can be accomplished when we work alone.

EXPERIENCE: Who could be on your team?

Spend some time reflecting on your congregation. Identify some of the people who could contribute to your church's mission and help you in ministry.

Assistant coach to you:

_____   _____   _____

_____   _____   _____

Lead a team or small group:

_____   _____   _____

_____   _____   _____

Perform a ministry task:

_____   _____   _____

_____   _____   _____

Assist or help someone in their ministry:

_____   _____   _____

_____   _____   _____

Not serving presently anywhere but with some encouragement or training they would:

_____   _____   _____

_____   _____   _____

CHAPTER 11

THE VALUE OF VALUES

Exodus 19-20

KEY PRINCIPLE: VALUES PROVIDE THE IMPORTANT "WHY" BEHIND WHAT WE DO!

"Jesus replied: 'Love the Lord your God with all your heart and with all your soul and with all your mind.' This is the first and greatest commandment.'"
—Matthew 22: 37-38

EXPOSURE: What are values?

In this chapter, we're going to discover the importance of values when leading toward God's vision. While we will be looking at values in this chapter, values were actually introduced in chapter 3, *The Power of Vision,* when we looked at the concept of a *vision frame.* The wise leader will early on in the change process identify the values of the congregation or organization and the values that will underpin the new vision to see where there may be conflict.

Let's begin with a working definition of values. Values can be simply defined as ***those things that are most important to us***! When you think about your personal values, those things that are most important to you, what comes to mind? Does family come to mind? Friends? Honesty? Integrity? Serving? Truth? God? Love? These are all examples of personal values.

Values are another way of looking at our deeply held personal beliefs, what we might call our *non-negotiables*. For a leader, values are especially important because our values end up being reflected in our priorities and values are the underpinning of a church's or organization's behavior.

Values are highly personal, and we attach great emotion to what we value. This is why discussion around values is where most conflict takes place when leading change.

The term *"values"* has some nuances that you'll want to be clear about. For instance, there is what is referred to as *espoused values*. Espoused values are the things we say are very important to us. These are the values that we say guide us or we think guide us. Espoused values are what we say we believe.

There is what is referred to as *aspired values*. Aspired values are the things that we hope will be reflected in our lives someday. These are the values we want to have, but currently lack. Aspired values are those values that do not currently exist within us or within our congregation, but to which we aspire. Aspired values remind us that we haven't arrived yet.

A third term is *functional* or *actual values*. Functional or actual values are those values we actually live out. These are the values we rely on to guide our decisions. Functional or actual values are the ones, which we personally own and act upon daily. Functional values are what we believe and actually live out.

One final term relevant to the discussion of values is what is called *shared values*. Shared values are those values that we agree upon as a family, as a team, or as a congregation. In relational environments, from families to companies to congregations, shared values provide the unwritten set of rules by which we've agreed to operate.

If we share a set of core values, then we can predict or count on one another's behaviors and thus feel safe. With shared values we have an understanding of what we will do and won't do, and how we will behave or not behave. Shared values, which people adhere to, provide that sense of belonging that helps us feel part of a group.

EXERCISE: *What do you personally value?*

Identify three of your espoused values: _____

_____

Identify three of your aspired values: _____

_____

Identify three of your functional or actual values: _____

_____

Identify three of your shared values you have with your family: _____

_____

EXPOSURE: *What does God value?*

"After they set out from Rephidim, they entered the Desert of Sinai, and Israel camped there in the desert in front of the mountain." (Exodus 19:2) Exodus nineteen opens in the shadow of Mount Sinai, the mountain where Moses had a very close encounter with God and where Moses would soon receive the Ten Commandments from God.

Most people, because they've watched Cecile B. DeMille's classic movie *The Ten Commandments*, probably believe that Moses climbed this mountain once and returned with the Ten Commandments. But look more closely and you'll see that Moses ascended Mount Sinai several times (19:3, 8, 20, 20:21, 24:12, 32:31, 34:1-2), which would have been challenging.

On the first trip up the mountain, God spoke this message to Moses for him to share with the people: *"³This is what you are to say to the descendants of Jacob and what you are to tell the people of Israel: ⁴ 'You yourselves have seen what I did to Egypt, and how I carried you on eagles' wings and brought you to myself. ⁵ Now if you obey me fully and keep my covenant, then out of all nations you will be my treasured possession. Although the whole earth is mine, ⁶ you will be for me a kingdom of priests and a holy nation.' These are the words you are to speak to the Israelites."* (Exodus 3:3-6)

Having heard from God, Moses descends the mountain and immediately summoned the elders of the people to tell them what God commanded. (Exodus 19:7). Why do you think he did this? Is it only a matter of honoring the elders as recognized leaders among the people? Or do you think that maybe it was to gain their support before telling the entire community. Certainly, once the elders accepted God's commandments, those who recognized the elders as their leaders would be more likely to embrace the commands. Getting buy-in from the elders would have given Moses leverage he needed to bring the people on board.

Getting your leaders on board before you make public announcements is a wise strategy for any leader. Winston Churchill, in a memorandum to his subordinate executives, once wrote: *"It is essential that you should beforehand give the decisions which will allow your lieutenants to act effectively."* (Hayward, *Churchill on Leadership*, pp.68-69)

Then Moses spoke all the words that God commanded him to the people. How did the people respond? *"The people all responded together, 'We will do everything the Lord has said.'" So, Moses brought their answer back to the Lord'"* (Exodus 19:8) Let me play their response back to you again. *"We will do everything the Lord has said!"*

In that moment, they covenanted with God. In that moment, everything changed for the Israelites—they were now expected to live by God's commandments, so that each Israelite had to understand and internalize these commandments. Moses ascended Mount Sinai a second time and brought their answer back to God. God said to Moses:

> *"⁹ I am going to come to you in a dense cloud, so that the people will hear me speaking with you and will always put their trust in you." Then Moses told the Lord what the people had said. ¹⁰ And the Lord said to Moses, "Go to the people and consecrate them today and tomorrow. Have them wash their clothes ¹¹ and be ready by the third day, because on that day the Lord will come down on Mount Sinai in the sight of all the people. ¹² Put limits for the people around the mountain and tell them, 'Be careful that you do not approach the mountain or touch the foot of it. Whoever touches the mountain is to be put to death. ¹³ They are to be stoned or shot with arrows; not a hand is to be laid on them. No person or animal shall be permitted to live.' Only when the ram's horn sounds a long blast may they approach the mountain." (Exodus 19:9-13)*

Moses went down the mountain and consecrated the people and had them clean their garments to reflect clean hearts. Moses erected clear boundaries to prevent the people from ascending Mount Sinai, or even touching it. God knew that they needed boundaries, and Moses accepted this and warned the people to be careful to not approach the mountain or touch the foot of it, because whoever touched the mountain would be put to death.

> **Exodus 19:16-25**
>
> *"¹⁶On the morning of the third day there was thunder and lightning, with a thick cloud over the mountain, and a very loud trumpet blast. Everyone in the camp trembled. ¹⁷Then Moses led the people out of the camp to meet with God, and they stood at the foot of the mountain. ¹⁸Mount Sinai was covered with smoke, because the Lord descended on it in fire. The smoke billowed up from it like smoke from a furnace, and the whole mountain trembled violently. ¹⁹As the sound of the trumpet grew louder and louder, Moses spoke and the voice of God answered him. ²⁰The Lord descended to the top of Mount Sinai and called Moses to the top of the mountain. So Moses went up ²¹and the Lord said to him, 'Go down and warn the people so they do not force their way through to see the Lord and many of them perish.²² Even*

> *the priests, who approach the Lord, must consecrate themselves, or the Lord will break out against them.' [23] Moses said to the Lord, 'The people cannot come up Mount Sinai, because you yourself warned us, 'Put limits around the mountain and set it apart as holy.' [24] The Lord replied, 'Go down and bring Aaron up with you. But the priests and the people must not force their way through to come up to the Lord, or he will break out against them.' [25] So Moses went down to the people and told them."*

The people waited at the base of Mount Sinai, while Moses ascended to the top. At the top of Mount Sinai, God descended to spoke to Moses what we have come to know as the Ten Commandments. God gave the people of Israel, through their leader Moses, a vision of where God ultimately was leading them, a Promise Land. But God's vision for Moses and the Israelites involved infinitely more than a just place. God's vision was spiritual. God's vision was a people who would love God and reflect God to the world as His Holy Nation.

In giving the Ten Commandments, God revealed of His own heart. God revealed what He values, and these things are not to be taken lightly. In the Ten Commandments, we see what God values in His people, that they would love Him and reflect Him to the world as His Holy nation. We see God's core values that were to define the character and culture of the Israelites and define their priorities.

What does God value? What were His BIG TEN values for the Israelites? On Mount Sinai, God spoke these BIG TEN values to His servant Moses:

1. *"Do not worship any other gods besides me."*
2. *"Do not make idols of any kind . . ."*
3. *"Do not misuse the name of the Lord your God . . ."*
4. *"Remember to observe the Sabbath day by keeping it holy . . ."* (Exodus 20:3-11)

What do these first four of the Ten Commandments reveal about what God values in our relationship with Him? God values uncompromised and undivided commitment to Himself. God values authentic commitment to Him. God values respect in our commitment to Him. God values a devotion to Him that is expressed in worship, where we rest from everything else to express the first-priority value we attach to God.

Jesus summarized these four commandments in what is often referred to as the Great Commandment. *"Hearing that Jesus had silenced the Sadducees, the Pharisees got together. One of them, an expert in the law, tested him with this question: 'Teacher, which is the greatest commandment in the Law?' Jesus replied: 'Love the Lord your God with all your heart and with all your soul and with all your mind.' This is the first and greatest commandment.'"* (Matthew 22: 34-38) In speaking the Great Commandment, Jesus expressed what God values.

God spoke these remaining commandments to Moses:

5. *"Honor your father and mother . . ."*
6. *"Do not murder."*
7. *"Do not commit adultery."*
8. *"Do not steal."*
9. *"Do not testify falsely against your neighbor."*
10. *"Do not covet your neighbor's house. Do not covet your neighbor's wife . . ."*

(Exodus 20:12-17)

The first four commandments focus on our relationship with God. The remaining six commandments focus on our relationship with people. The first four commandments have to do with our vertical relationship. The remaining six commandments focus on our horizontal relationships.

In these six commandments, God expressed the values that He expects from those who are His people. His values include things like: respect, love, faithfulness, trust and authenticity. What does each of the last six of the Ten Commandments reveal about what God values? All of these could be summarized in the one value of loving people!

Jesus summarizes these in Matthew 22:39-40, the second half of the Great Commandment, where Jesus speaks of the second greatest commandment. *"And the second is like it: Love your neighbor as yourself. All the Law and the Prophets hang on these two commandments.'"*

On Mount Sinai, God revealed His heart. God shared what He valued most in a community that was to be His Holy Nation. These values were given by God to shape the Israelites to be God's own people. God revealed His heart in His written Word. He took the time to inscribe it on stone. God took a chunk of Sinai stone and chiseled His revelation into it with his own finger. *"When the Lord finished speaking to Moses on Mount Sinai, he gave him the two tablets of the Testimony, the tablets of stone inscribed by the finger of God."* (Exodus 31:18)

EXERCISE: Values clarification

For this values clarification exercise, select your top five values from the list below. These will be the values that reflect where you actually spend the most amount of time, energy, and thought. After you have listed the top five, re-list them in order of priority as they show up in your life currently (not as you think they should show up). This is not a comprehensive list of values; if you have values that are not on this list, feel free to add them.

_____ Achievement	_____ Accountability/Responsibility
_____ Adventure	_____ Caring
_____ Balance	_____ Growth
_____ Beauty	_____ Communication
_____ Community	_____ Competency
_____ Contribution	_____ Respect

_____ Family   _____ Courage

_____ Freedom   _____ Creativity

_____ Friendship   _____ Discipline

_____ Bible   _____ Faith

_____ Health   _____ Fairness

_____ Justice   _____ Flexibility

_____ Love   _____ Forgiveness

_____ Nature/Environment   _____ Giving/Generosity

_____ Partnership/Collaboration   _____ Honesty

_____ Peace   _____ God/Christ

_____ Power   _____ Knowledge

_____ Recognition   _____ Loyalty

_____ Self-Worth   _____ Commitment

_____ Spirituality   _____ Truth

_____ Stability   _____ Grace

_____ Wealth   _____ Team

_____ Wisdom   _____ Friendship

_____ Diversity   _____ Sacrifice

_____ Respect   _____ Humor

_____ Trust   _____ People far from God

_____ Other _____   _____ Other _____

_____ Other _____   _____ Other _____

EXPOSURE: *What is the value of values?*

It is critical for leaders to grasp the importance of values because values explain why we do much of what we do. Values motivate us to behave in certain ways and are reflected in all our relationships. Our behaviors are a reflection of what is really important to us; in other words, our values.

To grasp this truth is to understand why congregations behave the way they do. Values explain why congregations do the things they do and why certain behaviors, practices, rituals, and traditions, are so deeply ingrained in the life of the congregation. They are so ingrained because they are valued!

When leading toward God's vision for your congregation, which will undoubtedly involve some change, the resistance you will experience will often be a result of challenging some congregational values. You will want to take time to identify congregational values so that you are aware of points of potential conflict.

For instance, if the congregation highly values stability, too much change or change brought on too quickly will likely create unnecessary conflict. Or, if a congregation does not have a high value on reaching spiritually lost people, then leading the congregation to reach out to the surrounding community will be much more challenging than if the congregation held a high value on reaching spiritually lost people.

Ask yourself, what does this congregation value? What is important to this congregation? But also help the congregation clarify its values. This is a highly spiritual process. It involves asking not just the question: What do you value? But a more important question: What does God value? Do your actions reflect those things God values?

What people value is very personal and highly emotional. As you clarify values and invite people to embrace values, expect conflict with those who have competing values. When you invite people to consider having their values subordinate to God's values, conflict will arise. The most volatile congregational conflicts surround the issue of values. So it is important that, as leader, you do the hard work of helping the congregation identify and clarify its values.

There is a very important relationship between vision and values. Vision and values go "hand-in-hand." You have been looking at leading your congregation toward God's vision. Vision defines WHERE we are heading. Remember our definition of vision? Vision is a clear mental picture of a preferred future. Vision has to do with our destination, where we are heading. As a leader, you ought to know where you are heading.

Values, on the other hand, define the *WHY* we are heading in the direction we are. Vision articulates *WHERE* you aspire to be. The purpose of clarifying your values is to help define *WHY* you are heading in the direction you are.

If you want to lead toward God's vision for your congregation, you will want to make sure that the congregation's vision and values are aligned. For when the congregation's values are in alignment with the vision the leader is casting, people will more likely be open to changes the vision might imply. As a leader, this means helping the congregation see that the vision is in alignment with what they value.

The congregation that I led for thirty years is over 125 years old. When I arrived, the congregation, like many older congregations was inward focused and in serious decline. To help the congregation embrace a vision for reaching spiritually lost people in our community, I attempted to connect the vision of reaching spiritually lost people to a value in the congregation that had long been forgotten.

I reminded the congregation often how the church began. I would tell the story of how on April 11, 1892, a railroad car named *Evangel* made history as it came into the lumber town of Everett, Washington to reach *"the lost."* The first church services were held in that railroad car. The name *Evangel* means *Good News.* For thirty years, I reminded the congregation how we began as a mission to reach the lumberjacks, drunkards and prostitutes of Everett, and that this was why God placed us in Everett.

When you connect a vision to reach spiritually lost people with a value like that, it motivates a congregation toward the vision. You see, our values are what motivates us to do what we do.

Think of values as the fuel, the passion that drives a congregation toward the vision. We are driven by our values. Values are, in fact, powerful drivers of how we think and behave. So, make the effort to connect values to vision.

Helping the entire congregation to connect values to the vision, which is helping them to understand why we do what we do, will serve as a glue for the congregation as it moves toward the vision. When a group of people hold common, shared values it is powerful glue for connecting people and providing people a sense of belonging and a sense of direction.

EXERCISE: Vision frame values

Take some time to reflect on the question, *"What does God value when it comes to His church?"* Return to your *vision frame* and see if you can come up with four or five values that are shared in your congregation. Be honest!

Vision Frame Values

1. _____

2. _____

3. _____

4. _____

5. _____

EXPERIENCE: *Plane crash*

This experience is an excellent creative problem solving and collaborative activity that requires a bit of imagination. Participants must pretend they are on a plane that has crashed on a deserted island and must choose items that would be most useful to aid in their survival. The items could include such items as: water, matches, knife, dental floss, rope, granola bar, fishhook, mirror, toilet paper. The assignment is for the team to come to a consensus on the ranking the importance of the items.

Chapter 12

COURAGEOUS LEADERSHIP

Exodus 32, Numbers 12 & 16

KEY PRINCIPLE: TOUGH CHALLENGES CALL FOR COURAGEOUS LEADERSHIP!

"You gain strength, courage and confidence by every experience in which you really stop to look fear in the face. You must do the thing you think you cannot do."
—Eleanor Roosevelt, former First Lady of the United States

EXPOSURE: *When there is a leadership vacuum*

Moses spent forty days on Mount Sinai in the presence of God receiving God's law, the commandments which he was to convey to the people. The people noticed that Moses delayed in coming down the mountain, and his absence troubled them and began to create insecurity.

"When the people saw that Moses was so long in coming down from the mountain, they gathered around Aaron and said, "Come, make us gods who will go before us. As for this fellow Moses who brought us up out of Egypt, we don't know what has happened to him." (Exodus 32:1)

Leadership vacuums are rife for dysfunction and disaster. When there is an absence of leadership, all kinds of personalities will vie for position, and not all the personalities will be qualified, have the purest motivation or be healthy. Perhaps because the people had become too dependent upon Moses, his absence created a leadership vacuum.

Their insecurity got the best of them and they demanded another leader to ensure that they would survive the desert journey. The actual request makes this clear: *"Come, make us elohim . . .* (usually understood as 'God') *who will go before us."* They wanted a replacement for Moses, who had disappeared.

They actually asked Aaron to provide them with *"gods"* (plural) who would show them the way in the desert. They reverted back to their experiences in Egypt where they had witnessed the worship of a multitude of tangible objects. In a sense, they had not yet weaned themselves from their attachment to Egypt. After 400 years of slavery in Egypt, ensconced in the adulterous practices of Egypt, the people had assimilated the religious culture of the surrounding society, and it was nearly impossible for them to abandon the known—the familiar religious practices—to worship *gods*.

Transformational change involves a long process. I'll say it again, *it took God only one night to get Israel out of Egypt, but it took 40 years for God to get Egypt out of Israel.* If you want to lead transformational change, you've got to be in for the long haul.

Instead of appointing a leader in Moses' place or assuming the role himself, Aaron fashioned a calf in response to the people's pleading for someone to lead them. Aaron, a peacemaker at heart, was incapable of making the tough decisions, that every leader must inevitably make, and gave into their demands. He was afraid and gave into their demands. Aaron went ahead and created a false and powerless symbol of leadership.

God saw what was happening at the foot of the mountain and told Moses, *"⁸ They have been quick to turn away from what I commanded them and have made themselves an idol cast in the shape of a calf. They have bowed down to it and sacrificed to it and have said, 'These are your gods, Israel, who brought you up out of Egypt.'* *9* *"I have seen these people,"* *the Lord said to Moses, "and they are a stiff-necked people.* *10* *Now leave* *me alone so that my anger may burn against them and that I may destroy* *them. Then I will make you into a great nation."* (Exodus 32:8-10)

God made it clear to Moses that what was happening below was no small thing. The people had cut a covenant with God. Do you remember their promise? *"We will do everything the Lord has said."* (Exodus 19:8) But here they were sacrificing to a golden calf with the commandment, *"Thou shalt have no other gods before Me"* freshly engraved on the tablet Moses held. They were not even close to behaving as God's people. Their sin was egregious and serious!

Perhaps sensing from God's words, *"Now leave me alone so that my* *anger may burn against them and that I may destroy them"* an opening to intercede on Israel's behalf Moses said to God:

> *"11 Why should your anger burn against your people, whom you brought out* *of Egypt with great power and a mighty hand? 12 Why should the Egyptians* *say, 'It was with evil intent that he brought them out, to kill them in the* *mountains and to wipe them off the face of the earth'? Turn from your* *fierce anger; relent and do not bring disaster on your people. 13 Remember* *your servants Abraham, Isaac and Israel, to whom you swore by your own* *self: 'I will make your descendants as numerous as the stars in the sky and* *I will give your descendants all this land I promised them, and it will be* *their inheritance forever.' 14 Then the Lord relented and did not bring on* *his people the disaster he had threatened."* (Exodus 32:11-14)

Interestingly, Moses chose to intercede on behalf of Israel. He implored God not to disown them; arguing that they would always be God's people. He pleaded with God not to give up on them, when God had already done so much for them, delivering them out of Egyptian slavery. Moses further defended his people by emphasizing that they had simply fallen back to old habits learned in Egypt and that God's expectations may have been a little unrealistic.

Leaders live in the tension between the ideal and the real. Leaders need to uphold the ideal—what God calls us to. But leaders must also recognize the reality of the lives of their people. It's the gap between their followers' potential and what can be realistically expected of them at any given time. The gap between the two—the ideal and the real— is bridged by patience.

Leadership requires patience, or *long suffering*. Leaders need to have patience with their followers, understanding that they have potential to grow with the necessary nurturing over time. It takes time and this requires a leader to be patient and gracious.

Other times what is needed is confrontation. Yet, how difficult it is for any leader to confront and deal with a stubbornly resistant group of followers, even when they reject essential values of the community. But to fail to confront or to be indecisive is always disastrous.

Exodus 32:15-20

"15 Moses turned and went down the mountain with the two tablets of the covenant law in his hands. They were inscribed on both sides, front and back. 16 The tablets were the work of God; the writing was the writing of God, engraved on the tablets. 17 When Joshua heard the noise of the people shouting, he said to Moses, "There is the sound of war in the camp." 18 Moses replied: "It is not the sound of victory, it is not the sound of defeat; it is the sound of singing that I hear." 19 When Moses approached the camp and saw the calf and the dancing, his anger burned and he threw the tablets out of his hands, breaking them to pieces at the foot of the mountain. 20 And he took the calf the people had made and burned it in the fire; then he ground it to powder, scattered it on the water and made the Israelites drink it."

Though he had been informed by God about what had been transpiring below, Moses could not have anticipated what he would see. Moses was stunned when he saw with his own eyes the deplorable actions of his people. Seeing his people dancing around the golden calf, he couldn't believe what he was seeing, and like God, his anger burned. Though he had defended them before God, now having witnessed the scene for himself, was the tipping point for Moses.

The site of such blatant pagan worship literally made him sick. The people were out of control. They had explicitly, publicly and completely broken their covenant with God, and as a result, Moses hurled the tablets upon which the Ten Commandments were written, shattering them. Just as the tablets lay broken, so was Moses.

Sometimes, situations call for patience and grace from a leader. Other times require decisive action. A leader cannot fail to address serious breaches regarding the community's shared values. Values are too important. A leader ignores serious breaches or violations of shared community values at his or her own peril.

Overlooking the egregious violation of their covenant to God would have seriously undercut Moses' leadership. If this kind of behavior was acceptable, then it would have raised all kinds of questions about what it meant to be God's people.

Though he realized the people were out of control, he gained enough composure to exercise leadership in what was a very difficult situation. This was one of the bigger tests of Moses' leadership. Norman Cohen writes, *"This may be his finest hour as a leader."* (Cohen, *Moses and the Journey to Leadership*, p. 118)

Moses mustered the courage to confront them and press for accountability. Even Aaron, and maybe especially Aaron, because Moses had empowered him as a leader to watch over the people had to accept accountability. He said to Aaron:

> [21] *"What did these people do to you, that you led them into such great sin?"* [22] *"Do not be angry, my lord," Aaron answered. "You know how prone these people are to evil.* [23] *They said to me, 'Make us gods who will go before us. As for this fellow Moses who brought us up out of Egypt, we don't know what has happened to him.'* [24] *So I told them, 'Whoever has any gold jewelry, take it off.' Then they gave me the gold, and I threw it into the fire, and out came this calf!" (Exodus 32:21-24)*

Leadership demands accountability if the goals and mission of the congregation or organization are to be fulfilled. At times this may be difficult to do when the leader is especially close to those who serve on the leadership team.

Then Moses looked to see that *"²⁵the people were running wild and that Aaron had let them get out of control and so become a laughingstock to their enemies. ²⁶ So he stood at the entrance to the camp and said, 'Whoever is for the Lord, come to me.' And all the Levites rallied to him."* (Exodus 32:25-26)

Sometimes a leader must draw a line in the sand, and call people to take a stand. But leaders need to be wise about this. Not everything deserves *a line in the sand.* Leaders need to ask themselves, *"Is this important enough to draw a line? Is this a hill worth dying for?"*

I've learned over the many years I've led in the church, that there are only few things I was willing to die for. Not every issue is an essential issue. However, non-negotiable, community-shared values are one of the things that require drawing a line in the sand.

Courageously, Moses cried out, *"Whoever is for the Lord, come to me."* And all the Levites rallied to him. What Moses did in drawing the line in the sand, was to establish his base of support as the Levites rallied around him and dedicated themselves to God. As a leader, sometimes you just need to know who is *"all in"* and who is not.

EXERCISE: Line in the sand

Write one thing for which you would draw a line in the sand.

_____

_____

_____

_____

_____

_____

_____

_____

_____

EXPOSURE: *Accountability*

Opposing Moses, and God, were all those who consciously and deliberately chose to not stand with Moses. They chose not to be God's people. Part of Moses' leadership responsibility was to set consequences for those who clamored for the building of the calf in direct violation of the commandments and the values of the community, and refused to repent.

> [27] *Then he said to them, "This is what the Lord, the God of Israel, says: 'Each man strap a sword to his side. Go back and forth through the camp from one end to the other, each killing his brother and friend and neighbor.'"* [28] *The Levites did as Moses commanded, and that day about three thousand of the people died.* [29] *Then Moses said, "You have been set apart to the Lord today, for you were against your own sons and brothers, and he has blessed you this day."* [30] *The next day Moses said to the people, "You have committed a great sin. But now I will go up to the Lord; perhaps I can make atonement for your sin."* [31] *So Moses went back to the Lord and said, "Oh, what a great sin these people have committed! They have made themselves gods of gold.* [32] *But now, please forgive their sin—but if not, then blot me out of the book you have written."* [33] *The Lord replied to Moses, "Whoever has sinned against me I will blot out of my book. (Exodus 32:27-33)*

Moses understood that the punishment to be meted out had to be severe if the people were to be shaped into a community that lived out the values. Leadership must demand accountability, especially when it comes to the values of the community.

EXERCISE: Accountability

Identify one aspect of accountably in your church or organization.

_____

_____

_____

_____

_____

_____

EXPOSURE: When your leadership is challenged

You cannot help getting the sense that Moses felt over-burdened when you read Numbers 11:11-15.

> *[11] He asked the Lord, "Why have you brought this trouble on your servant? What have I done to displease you that you put the burden of all these people on me? [12] Did I conceive all these people? Did I give them birth? Why do you tell me to carry them in my arms, as a nurse carries an infant, to the land you promised on oath to their ancestors? [13] Where can I get meat for all these people? They keep wailing to me, 'Give us meat to eat!' [14] I cannot carry all these people by myself; the burden is too heavy for me. [15] If this is how you are going to treat me, please go ahead and kill me—if I have found favor in your eyes—and do not let me face my own ruin."*

Moses' energy was ebbing. Feeling overburdened by the people, he began to distance himself from the people in order to protect himself. But it is never a good thing for a leader to isolate himself or herself.

As a result of isolating himself, Miriam and Aaron felt free to criticize their younger brother. Chapter 12, in the book of Numbers, begins, *"Miriam and Aaron began to talk against Moses because of his Cushite wife, for he had married a Cushite."* Note that they spoke, not just *"about*

Moses" but, *"against Moses,"* indicating the toxic nature of their criticism of their brother and leader.

Miriam and Aaron began murmuring against Moses because he had married a Cushite. In other words, she was a non-Israelite. She is referenced as a Cushite, which may imply that she was dark-skinned or perhaps beautiful like women in Ethiopia.

But this was only the presenting issue, not the real issue. The real issue? Read the second verse of Numbers 12: *"2 Has the Lord spoken only through Moses?" they asked. "Hasn't he also spoken through us?" And the Lord heard this."* At first hearing, this sounds like a case of jealousy. But there is more at play here. This is a power struggle, and if you are in leadership long enough, you will encounter one.

They were making the case that Moses was not the only one God had spoken through; God had spoken just as much through them. Moses was forced to confront the challenge of maintaining his leadership position, in this case, with his family. This is especially difficult for leaders who are younger siblings.

While often surrounded by individuals who play important leadership roles, it is crucial for the point leader's distinctiveness to be recognized by all. Each person's contribution should be valued. But when confronted by those who think they can take charge and take over in the same way as the leader, the leader needs to demonstrate the qualities that distinguishes her or him as *"the leader of leaders."*

Perhaps Miriam and Aaron had simply gotten the wrong impression of Moses as he isolated himself. Perhaps they interpreted it as Moses thinking of himself as better than them. In any case, in response to Miriam and Aaron's criticism of Moses, God immediately came to Moses' defense. Before He did, there is a description of Moses that may be an attempt to explain what's going on with Moses. Numbers 12:3

read: *"³ (Now Moses was a very humble man, more humble than anyone else on the face of the earth.)"*

Patrick Lencioni, a noted management consultant, stresses that even though leaders need to be charismatic in order to succeed, they also need to be humble. In his view, humility means that leaders know that they are inherently no better than the people they lead and must not distance themselves from them. (Patrick Lencioni, *"The Trouble with Humility," Leader to Leader* (Winter 919): 44.)

Perhaps it was Moses' humility that kept him from lashing out at his siblings. As hurtful as Miriam's remarks were to Moses, he restrained himself. Occasionally, as we have seen, Moses did respond angrily when his leadership was challenged. This time, however, humility won the day.

But God immediately came to Moses' defense. Such a challenge to his leadership could not go unaddressed. Clarity had to be brought to who was *the leader of the leaders.* God's *"at once"* response is found in Numbers 12:4-10.

"⁴At once the Lord said to Moses, Aaron and Miriam, "Come out to the tent of meeting, all three of you." So the three of them went out. ⁵ Then the Lord came down in a pillar of cloud; he stood at the entrance to the tent and summoned Aaron and Miriam. When the two of them stepped forward, ⁶ he said, "Listen to my words:
"When there is a prophet among you,
I, the Lord, reveal myself to them in visions,
I speak to them in dreams.
⁷ But this is not true of my servant Moses;
he is faithful in all my house.
⁸ With him I speak face to face,
clearly and not in riddles;
he sees the form of the Lord.
Why then were you not afraid
to speak against my servant Moses?"

> *⁹ The anger of the Lord burned against them, and he left them. ¹⁰ When the cloud lifted from above the tent, Miriam's skin was leprous—it became as white as snow. Aaron turned toward her and saw that she had a defiling skin disease."*

Miriam is punished with some sort of skin disease, as it seems she was the principle instigator of the gossip against her brother. However, Aaron's sense of guilt and conviction comes through his own confession to Moses: *"¹¹Please, my lord, I ask you not to hold against us the sin we have so foolishly committed. ¹² Do not let her be like a stillborn infant coming from its mother's womb with its flesh half eaten away."*

The humility of Moses is seen again as Moses interceded for her healing. *"¹³Moses cried out to the LORD, 'Please, God, heal her!'"*

To succeed, leaders can't hold on to their hurts. Leaders must learn to move beyond their personal hurt and rejection, to continue acting on behalf of all their followers, even those who have hurt them. Though he was hurt by his siblings' comments, Moses moved beyond any feelings of animosity or need for *reprisal*. He not only prayed on their behalf, but also forgave them. Wise leaders discipline themselves to keep a short list of offenses. Resentment and bitterness drain a leader of the energy they need to lead.

As a result of Moses' intercession, Miriam was only quarantined, or shut out of the Israelite camp, for seven days due to her skin disease. She was isolated from the people. Sometimes, when leaders act inappropriately, they do not deserve to maintain their position of leadership. In fact, being asked to step away from leadership responsibilities for a season could be one of the healthiest things for both the offending leader and the community.

All of us, but especially leaders, should keep in mind that people are human, and occasionally act inappropriately. Like Moses, all leaders must find ways to stay humble, yet engaged, especially when their leadership is challenged. What can help us as leaders is remembering that we, too, are human and make mistakes.

EXPOSURE: *When facing all-out rebellion*

The challenge Moses faced from his siblings pales in comparison to the rebellion led by Korah, Dathan, Abiram and their supporters we read about in Numbers 16 and Numbers 17:1-6. This coup to undermine the leadership of Moses threatened the very success of the journey toward God's vision of the Promise Land.

At one point or another, every leader will face a moment like this, which will test the leader's courage. Jack Welch, former CEO of General Electric, once said, *"Leaders have the courage to make unpopular decisions and gut calls."*

What made this rebellion more threatening was that it involved many factions coming together in their opposition to Moses' and Aaron's leadership. The focus of their criticism was Moses' and Aaron's authority, and the lack of success of their leadership in general. Here is how Numbers 16 begins:

> *"[1] Korah son of Izhar, the son of Kohath, the son of Levi, and certain Reubenites—Dathan and Abiram, sons of Eliab, and On son of Peleth— became insolent [2] and rose up against Moses. With them were 250 Israelite men, well-known community leaders who had been appointed members of the council. [3] They came as a group to oppose Moses and Aaron and said to them, "You have gone too far! The whole community is holy, every one of them, and the Lord is with them. Why then do you set yourselves above the Lord's assembly?"*

They came as a group to oppose Moses and Aaron. The people seemed to have agreed with the claim that both Moses and Aaron had relegated to themselves too much power and authority. Some commentators believe that Korah's jealousy was directed against the choice of Aaron, Moses' brother, as high priest. Nepotism might have been his concern. Korah, who appears to be the ringleader, questioned Moses' appointment of his own brother for the priesthood.

Co-conspirators, Dathan and Abiram, further capitalized on the challenging times the Israelites faced and the Israelites' intense bitterness. *"13 Isn't it enough that you have brought us up out of a land flowing with milk and honey to kill us in the wilderness? And now you also want to lord it over us!"* (Numbers 16:13)

This was an all-out rebellion. As we read at the beginning of the chapter, in addition to Korah, Dathan and Abiram, *"250 well-known community leaders came as a group to oppose Moses and Aaron." Several times in the narrative, Korah is said to have "gathered all his followers in opposition to them"* (Numbers 16:19) or the people are *"gathered against Moses and Aaron"* Some of the people became so convinced by Korah that they wanted to stone Moses.

Let's look closely at how Moses handled this. When first charged with *going too far*, of setting himself up above the Lord's assembly, Moses *"fell facedown."* Sometimes leaders face situations that can knock the wind out of our sail or knock us to the ground.

Moses probably understood at this point that Korah and his followers had to be confronted head on. This was not a time to retreat, to isolate or to stay on the ground. It was time to confront.

Note that Moses confronted them in person. Individuals who use a group to advance their counter-productive agendas must be stopped, and the leader must have the courage to act because of the serious damage they can do to the whole group. This especially applies to influential members of the group.

Moses spoke first directly to Korah and his followers. He suggested that they determine to let the Lord decide who belonged to him, who was holy and who was to lead. Moses said: *"⁵ In the morning the Lord will show who belongs to him and who is holy, and he will have that person come near him. The man he chooses he will cause to come near him. ⁶ You, Korah, and all your followers are to do this: Take censers ⁷ and tomorrow put burning coals and incense in them before the Lord. The man the Lord chooses will be the one who is holy.* Then courageously he does not back down but adds, *"⁷ You Levites have gone too far!"*

Moses also said to Korah, *"⁸ Now listen, you Levites! ⁹ Isn't it enough for you that the God of Israel has separated you from the rest of the Israelite community and brought you near himself to do the work at the Lord's tabernacle and to stand before the community and minister to them? ¹⁰ He has brought you and all your fellow Levites near himself, but now you are trying to get the priesthood too. ¹¹ It is against the Lord that you and all your followers have banded together."* (Numbers 16:8-11)

Moses asked them why they were not satisfied with their position and why did they felt they needed to demand the high priesthood. What Moses was doing was exposing their *"power grab."* And then, to help them see the seriousness of their offense, he charged them, *"¹¹ It is against the Lord that you and all your followers have banded together."* Korah did not even acknowledge Moses' pleas; he never uttered a word.

Moses then summoned Dathan and Abiram. But they said, *"¹²We will not come!"* Dathan and Abiram refused to meet with Moses. Despite Moses' efforts at reconciliation, none of the rebels responded to him.

What did Moses do? Moses turned to God and cried out, *"Do not accept their offering. I have not taken so much as a donkey from them, nor have I wronged any of them."* (Numbers 16:15) Moses pled with God to reject their sacrifices.

Though angered by their words, Moses did not let the strife escalate. One of the traits of successful leaders is the ability to let go of any malice or enmity they might feel toward those who oppose them, recognizing that reconciliation better serves the needs of the people and advances of the mission.

> *Then Moses said to Korah, "¹⁶ You and all your followers are to appear before the Lord tomorrow—you and they and Aaron. ¹⁷ Each man is to take his censer and put incense in it—250 censers in all—and present it before the Lord. You and Aaron are to present your censers also." ¹⁸ So each of them took his censer, put burning coals and incense in it, and stood with Moses and Aaron at the entrance to the tent of meeting. ¹⁹ When Korah had gathered all his followers in opposition to them at the entrance to the tent of meeting, the glory of the Lord appeared to the entire assembly. ²⁰ The Lord said to Moses and Aaron, ²¹ "Separate yourselves from this assembly so I can put an end to them at once." ²² But Moses and Aaron fell facedown and cried out, "O God, the God who gives breath to all living things, will you be angry with the entire assembly when only one man sins?" ²³ Then the Lord said to Moses, ²⁴ "Say to the assembly, 'Move away from the tents of Korah, Dathan and Abiram.'" (Numbers 16:16-24)*

The rebellion of Korah, Dathan and Abiram was a disease that threatened the life of the entire community. So, Moses warned the rebellious people who had joined them, though he doesn't do it alone at this point. Note that Moses gathered the elders of the community with him.

"²⁵ Moses got up and went to Dathan and Abiram, and the elders of Israel followed him. ²⁶ He warned the assembly, "Move back from the tents of these wicked men! Do not touch anything belonging to them, or you will be swept away because of all their sins." ²⁷ So they moved away from the tents of Korah, Dathan and Abiram. Dathan and Abiram had come out and were standing with their wives, children and little ones at the entrances to their tents." (Numbers 16:25-27)

Sometimes dysfunctional conflict can escalate to where there may come a time that, for the sake of the group, termination is the only option. You never want to choose this option too quickly out of anger and frustration. But if you take the steps toward reconciliation, and the response is a defiant unwillingness to work toward reconciliation, leaders must have the courage to discipline rebelliousness.

In Matthew 18:15-17, Jesus prescribed these steps for working toward reconciliation: *"15 "If your brother or sister sins, go and point out their fault, just between the two of you. If they listen to you, you have won them over. 16 But if they will not listen, take one or two others along, so that 'every matter may be established by the testimony of two or three witnesses.' 17 If they still refuse to listen, tell it to the church; and if they refuse to listen even to the church, treat them as you would a pagan or a tax collector."*

The steps toward reconciliation include:

1. Go first to the person and seek to address the conflict. Keep the matter between the two of you.
2. If that is not successful in bringing reconciliation, take one or two impartial others.
3. If the person refuses to listen, tell it to the church.
4. If they still refuse to listen and continue their rebellious behavior, see them as you would someone outside the community who doesn't yet believe in God.

These are the steps that Moses took. So, following Moses's public warning and plea, the entire nation knew that those who rebelled were spurned by God. There must have been a sense that God was going to do something dramatic, and dramatic it was. Suddenly, *"31 as soon as he finished saying all this, the ground under them split apart 32 and the earth opened its mouth and swallowed them and their households, and all those associated with Korah, together with possessions. 33 They went down alive into the realm of the dead, with everything they owned; the earth closed over them, and they perished and were gone from the community."* (Numbers 16:31-33) The punishment was so dramatic that it left an indelible impression on the people as a whole.

Unfortunately, the discontent aroused by the rebels had inflicted damage on the community. Korah's actions undermined those leaders chosen by God, and the effect would be evidenced in further division and complaining for years to come.

This is another of the challenges of leadership. Leaders are always challenged to gauge the long-term damage that rebellious actions can have upon the community as a whole against the short-term pain that confronting extreme inappropriate behavior may cause.

Sometimes challenges to our leadership require us to be still, to just wait and see. At other times challenges to our leadership require us to go to the person, one on one, to seek reconciliation. Or if that doesn't work, we would be wise to invite others into the process in order to confront inappropriate behavior. Unfortunately, sometimes the only option is termination because the very values of the community are being challenged. It all comes down to judgement; and then the courage to do what you've judged to be the right thing to do.

EXPERIENCE: *Your biggest leadership conflict*

Write about your biggest leadership conflict that required you to be courageous. Then gather in a group of 3-4 other leaders together where you can all share your biggest leadership conflict stories.

_____

_____

_____

_____

_____

_____

_____

_____

CHAPTER 13

THE CHARACTER OF THE LEADER

Numbers 20:1-13; 21:16-19

KEY PRINCIPLE: CHARACTER IS EVERYTHING!

"Your success stops where your character stops. You can never rise above the limitations of your character."
—John Maxwell

EXPOSURE: *Self Leadership*

One aspect of leadership that is often overlooked is SELF-LEADERSHIP. Yet, the greatest leadership failures often come as a result of poor self-leadership.

The primary focus of self-leadership is one's character. What is character? Character is the sum of the qualities that make us who we are. As often said, character is who we are in the dark, or who we are when no one is looking. Our character goes deeper than our performance. While performance is about what we do and how well we do, character is who we really are.

For the spiritual leader, Godly character must be a priority of the highest order. What provides us any sense of authority, as spiritual leaders, is our personal and intimate relationship with God. This was true for Moses, and it is true for us.

We pick up our story in Numbers 20 where we learn that *"in the first month the whole Israelite community arrived at the Desert of Zin, and they stayed at Kadesh. There Miriam died and was buried."* (Numbers 20:1) Moses and Aaron immediately began to mourn for their older sibling.

But the people appear to be insensitive to the sorrow that Moses and Aaron were experiencing. The people came to them, not to pay their respects to the brothers nor to Miriam, but rather to complain once again about the lack of water. To add insult to injury, they spoke of Egypt as this luxuriant place. After a journey of nearly forty years, where they had repeatedly witnessed God's redemptive hand, they appeared to not have internalized much of God's power and provision on their behalf.

It hard to imagine what it must have been like for Moses and Aaron to hear the people's tirade one more time, especially in their fragile emotional state. But leaders must find the strength to weather personal attacks and continue to help their followers grow and realize their potential. This is especially challenging when leaders are suffering their own personal crisis, and even grief.

These two leaders, *"⁶ Moses and Aaron went from the assembly to the entrance to the tent of meeting and fell facedown, and the glory of the LORD appeared to them."* (Numbers 20:6) These two leaders had literally been sapped of their strength, having lost their patience and perhaps even their resolve. Their impulse was to withdraw and even hide from the Israelites with their constant complaints so that they could mourn their sister's death.

But leadership responsibilities did not allow them the luxury of abandoning their leadership role, as God commanded them to take up the rod, the symbol of God's presence and power, and assemble the people. God commanded, *"8 "Take the staff, and you and your brother Aaron gather the assembly together. Speak to that rock before their eyes and it will pour out its water. You will bring water out of the rock for the community so they and their livestock can drink." (Numbers 20: 8)*

At Rephidim, near the outset of the journey (Exodus 17), God commanded Moses to strike the rock with the rod to produce life-giving water for the people. However, here at Kadesh, God commanded Moses to *"speak to the rock in the presence of the people."*

Moses took the rod and said to the gathered assembly, *"10 Listen, you rebels, must we bring you water out of this rock?"* (Numbers 20:10) You can hear the tone in his voice. Suffering from the death of his sister, Miriam, and being unable to mourn for her, and having lost patience with the people's incessant complaining, Moses lashed out at the people, referring to them as *"morim,"* a word understood either as *"rebels"* or *"fools."* The choice of words is very revealing of Moses' emotional state.

In the moment, Moses projected onto the Israelites all his frustration and anger because of their constant complaining and Miriam's death, which they appeared to not care much about. Unable to control his emotions, *"11 Moses raised his arm and struck the rock twice with his staff. Water gushed out, and the community and their livestock drank."* (Numbers 20:11)

Though he had been told to speak to the rock, Moses took matters literally into his own hands and struck the rock, and the reader can feel his anger and rage. His emotions overtook him. Leaders must strive to control their emotions, despite what they might be feeling in order to fulfill their larger role. However, being able to refrain from allowing our personal feelings to color our decision making is an especially difficult challenge at times.

Though the water came forth from the rock, God chastised both Moses and Aaron, saying, *"12 "Because you did not trust in me enough to honor me as holy in the sight of the Israelites, you will not bring this community into the land I give them."* (Numbers 20:12)

Moses acted contrary to God's command in the sight of all the people. This was serious. The people could have begun to feel that, if their leaders could do this, so could they. Leaders must realize that every one of their public actions must be seriously weighed because of how it can affect their followers. Leaders are considered models, and therefore everything they say and do will be scrutinized by their followers. Every single word uttered by Moses and Aaron, let alone any of their individual acts, had the potential to either enhance God's sanctity in the eyes of the people or diminish it.

In the end, the core reason Moses was forbidden to lead the people of Israel in the land of promise was because he demonstrated that he no longer had the ability to do so. His capacity to lead had been diminished, along with his authority. Even Moses did not receive special treatment, when he acted in a willful, rebellious way. He failed to model the highest values to which every Israelite had been called. In the end, all of us are accountable for our actions, especially leaders.

Interestingly, the place where all this transpires is named Kadesh, or *Holy Place*. Ironically, it is at this Holy Place where Moses commits this unholy act. Have you learned yet that places of adversity in our own journey can expose our character, along with character flaws, like no other place?

Some places are more challenging than others. In recovery, there is an acronym used to identify those places that are most dangerous to the soul, when we can be more susceptible than other times to slipping up. The acronym is *H.A.L.T.* We are most vulnerable to falling into temptation when we are:

- **HUNGRY**—When we hunger after things, or are starving for attention, or have an insatiable appetite for the things of this world, we are spiritually vulnerable. Our cravings and needs can draw anyone of us to dark places.

- **ANGRY**—Our anger, or other emotions, can fuel us and drive us in unhealthy directions. Moses always had an anger problem. We saw it back in Egypt when he killed an Egyptian. We saw it along the journey when Moses became angry at the Israelites because of their constant complaining. The cauldron of unresolved anger boiled over here at Kadesh. Because of his unwillingness to have his passion and anger shaped by God, God determined there at Kadesh that Moses would not have the privilege of leading the people of Israel into the Promise Land.

- **LONELY**—When we isolate ourselves and disconnect from Christian fellowship, we make ourselves vulnerable to our spiritual enemy, who prowls around like a hungry lion waiting to devour us. Isolation can delude us into thinking that we are responsible for carrying the full weight of leadership by ourselves or imagining we are not accountable to anyone.

- **TIRED**—Our energy is not limitless, and yet leaders often over-commit and over-work to a point of exhaustion. When our energy is low, when we are tired, we are vulnerable to mistakes we would never make if we were not so exhausted.

EXERCISE: Dangerous wilderness places

Read the story of Jesus' own temptation in *the wilderness* found in Matthew 4:1-11 and write down what you learn about temptation in *dangerous wilderness places*.

_____

_____

_____

_____

_____

_____

_____

_____

_____

EXPOSURE: *Spiritual Disciplines*

One of the commitments that can help a leader grow in Godly character is what is called *spiritual disciplines*. *Spiritual disciplines* or *spiritual exercises* are like physical exercises in that the more we do them, the stronger we become in our character. There are several spiritual disciplines, too many for me to identify and write about. But let me identify five key disciplines for the character development of the leader.

- **Prayer**—It is hard to overestimate the importance of this spiritual discipline for the leader. 1 Thessalonians 5:17 calls us to *"pray continually"* or *"pray without ceasing."* Romans 12:12 calls us to be *"faithful in prayer."* Philippians 4:6 says, *"Do not be anxious about anything, but in every situation, by prayer and petition, with thanksgiving, present your requests to God."*

Prayer is simply asking God for help, strength, and provision. But prayer is infinitely more than asking God for things. Prayer is this conversation with God where we become intimately acquainted with God, to even know His heart.

- **Meditation on God's Word**—The Psalmist wrote, *"I have hidden your word in my heart that I might not sin against you."* (Psalm 119:1) Facing His own temptation, Jesus said to the Tempter, *"It is written: 'Man shall not live on bread alone, but on every word that comes from the mouth of God.'"*

The Word of God provides us truth and guidance as leaders. Spiritual leaders must be persons of the Word, and we become persons of the Word by meditation. To *"meditate"* on God's word means to ponder it, dwell on it, chew on it and roll it over in our minds in order to apply it to our lives. Two ways we can do this are to read or listen to God's word and memorize it.

- **Fellowship**—Isolation makes a leader vulnerable to falling into temptation. A leader, to be at his or her best, should be connected to others in fellowship that involves accountability to leaders who are better or further ahead than you.

- **Sabbath**—Rest is a gracious gift from God for the weary. Jesus said, *"Come to me, all you who are weary and burdened, and I will give you rest."* (Matthew 11:28) Practicing sabbath is disengaging from the work of ministry for rest and replenishment. In resting from our labor, we define ourselves, not by what we do, but by who we are as children of God. While Sabbath in the Old Testament refers specifically to Saturday, our Sabbath could be any day of the week where we rest from our labor.

- **Stewardship**—Scripture calls us to generosity. 1 Corinthians 16:2 says, *"On the first day of every week, each one of you should set aside a sum of money in keeping with your income, saving it up, so that when I come no collections will have to be made."* Proverbs 19:17 says, "Whoever is kind to the poor lends to the Lord, and he will reward them for what they have done." Jesus said: *"Give, and it will be given to you. A good measure, pressed down, shaken together and running over, will be poured into your lap. For with the measure you use, it will be measured to you."* Jesus commands us to give. It is in a sense, a *"spiritual discipline."* But it brings great rewards, as Jesus said.

EXERCISE: Spiritual Disciplines

What spiritual disciplines do you regularly practice?

- Prayer _____
- Fasting _____
- Meditation on God's Word _____
- Fellowship _____
- Worship _____
- Sabbath _____
- Stewardship _____
- Celebration _____
- Thanksgiving _____
- Service _____
- Chastity _____
- _____

EXPOSURE: Boundaries

A second commitment that can help a leader grow in Godly character and maintain Godly character is establishing healthy *boundaries*. What are boundaries? And what does it mean to establish healthy boundaries in one's life?

Think of boundaries as *guardrails for your spiritual journey*. Guardrails are not found every place along a highway. Normally, guardrails are placed at the most dangerous places along the highway such as at a curve or at the edge of a cliff. Guardrails are meant to remind drivers to be careful; do not come too close. You don't drive as close as you can to a guardrail. You try to keep some distance between you and the guardrail knowing that danger is on the other side of the guardrail.

In the same way, we establish boundaries and self-imposed *"guardrails"* in our lives at places where we could easily go off the righteous path. Three dangerous places that are common traps for leaders are money, power, or pride. In a *Time* magazine article, Billy Graham once commented that Satan attacks God's servants in the three areas of sex, money, and pride.

In 1948, 31-year-old Billy Graham was coming off a successful stint as a Youth for Christ evangelist and entering a period of independent ministry that would last almost six decades. His revival team included Bev Shea, Grady Wilson, and Cliff Barrows. The quartet was young and charismatic.

But Graham had observed the failure of other ministers and evangelists, and so to guard against allegations or the actual abuse of money, sex, and power that had felled previous evangelists, the Graham team decided to take concrete steps to avoid the slightest whiff of controversy.

The team gathered in a hotel room in Modesto, California. They drew up a compact that became known as the *"Modesto Manifesto,"* though they produced no written document. The manifesto included provisions for handling money raised by offerings and financial accountability. These policies would help Graham and his team avoid charges of financial exploitation and hucksterism.

Related to the temptation of sexual immorality, the most famous provision of the manifesto called for each man on the Graham team never to be alone with a woman other than his wife. Graham, from that day forward, pledged not to eat, travel, or meet with a woman other than Ruth unless other people were present. This commitment enabled Graham and his team to dodge accusations that had waylaid evangelists before and since.

As to the temptation of pride, Graham recognized that we, who are called to lead others, by our very natures, have healthy egos. We enjoy the spotlight and the accolades. The challenge for us is to maintain a sense of humility, which is crucial if we are to truly succeed as servant leaders. One of the reasons God was able to use Moses was his humility. *"Moses was a very humble man, more so than any other person on the earth."* Numbers 12:3 Humility is the antidote to power and pride.

Pride deludes us into thinking we are better than we are and that we could never fall into temptation. But 1 Corinthians 10:12-13 cautions us: *"¹² So, if you think you are standing firm, be careful that you don't fall! ¹³ No temptation has overtaken you except what is common to mankind. And God is faithful; he will not let you be tempted beyond what you can bear. But when you are tempted, he will also provide a way out so that you can endure it."* Imagining that we are above temptation, thinking that it could never happen to us, makes us most susceptible to falling into temptation.

Gordon MacDonald was a pastor of one of America's leading churches and president of Intervarsity Christian Fellowship when his world came down due to an adulterous relationship. In his book *Building Below the Waterline: Shoring Up the Foundations of Leadership*, he writes:

> *"In my book, Rebuilding Your Broken World, I told the story of a man I met at a conference. I could tell he was trying to create conversation as he asked: 'How do you think Satan could blow you out of the water?' I was a younger man at the time, and I had no quick answer. So I said I'm not sure, but I am confident that he could never get at me by undermining my personal relationships. I could hardly have said a more foolish thing. A few years later, I was a potential DNF, (Did Not Finish), and it was reasonable to ask if I would ever "race" again. Why? For a moment, I had failed in the one human relationship most important to me."* (Gordon MacDonald, *Building Below the Waterline: Shoring Up the Foundations of Leadership*, pp. 160-161)

The one thing Gordon MacDonald had prided himself in not doing, he ended up doing. So, *"if you are standing firm, thinking it could never happen to you, be careful that you don't fall."* This is why healthy boundaries are so important.

EXERCISE: *If you think you are standing firm*

"How do you think Satan could blow you out of the water?"

_____

_____

_____

_____

_____

_____

_____

EXERCISE: *Putting it into practice*

What spiritual discipline or boundary would be most relevant to you?

_____

_____

_____

_____

_____

_____

_____

EXPERIENCE: *Magic flying carpet*

Start with a small tarp or rug that allows all the group members to be able to stand on. Tell the group that they are now on a magic flying carpet and cannot step off. The group must work as a team to flip the tarp or rug over without having anyone step off. If a group member falls off the magic flying carpet, the team must start over.

CHAPTER 14

SUCCESSORS TO THE LEADER

Deuteronomy 31:1-8

KEY PRINCIPLE: THERE IS NO SUCCESS WITHOUT A SUCCESSOR!

"Succession is one of the key responsibilities of leadership."
—Max Dupree, *Leadership Is an Art*

EXPOSURE: If you were hit by a bus . . .

One of the issues you must give high priority to as a leader is identifying, recruiting and developing the people around you. To bring a sense of priority or urgency to this issue, consider this question: *If you were hit by a bus and found yourself in the hospital for weeks, who would fill your shoes?*

Are you developing the leaders around you, especially the leader or leaders who will replace you? Here is the Big Idea for this lesson: Without a successor, there can be no real long-term success! Max Dupree, author of *Leadership Is an Art*, declared, *"Succession is one of the key responsibilities of leadership."*

Imagine a relay team running a 4x100 race. During the first leg of the race, the first member of the team sets a leading pace and passes off the baton to the second runner who holds the pace. The third runner, upon receiving the baton from the second runner, extends the lead and heads to the final runner. As the third runner is passing the baton to the fourth and final runner, the baton slips out of her hand and falls to the ground. The fourth runner quickly grabs the baton up off the ground and runs toward the finish line. Though the team had the lead most of the race, they ended up losing the race because of the failure to successfully pass the baton in the last leg of the race.

Can you imagine leading an effort, leading it well over years, only to see the effort fail because after you left, the next leader dropped the baton? Sometimes the failure of leadership is in the passing of the baton from one leader to the next. I learned this the hard way. Because the first church I pastored in Toledo, Ohio grew very quickly I thought I was successful. When I started my ministry there in Toledo, we had only 35 people attending. Over the five years I served there, the congregation grew as we reached out into the community. We constructed a new sanctuary and when I left, our attendance was over two hundred.

A few years ago, my wife and I were invited back for that church's fiftieth anniversary, only to learn that the church was not doing very well, and that the congregation had decided to close its doors. I can't tell you how much this saddened me. My wife and I had put a lot of ourselves into that first church. But obviously I had not prepared the church to succeed after I left.

A time comes in our leadership when we need to delegate ministry to others and eventually pass off the leadership baton to someone else. The question we need to ask is, have we developed the people around us to be capable leaders in our absence or even to replace us?

Moses did not enjoy the privilege of leading the people of Israel into the Promise Land, because Moses broke trust with God. Moses died in the desert. But before he died, God made Moses aware of the need for a successor, someone who would lead in Moses' place. The public announcement of Moses' successor comes in Deuteronomy 31:7-8.

> "Then Moses summoned Joshua and said to him in the presence of all Israel, "Be strong and courageous, for you must go with this people into the land that the LORD swore to their forefathers to give them, and you must divide it among them as their inheritance. The LORD himself goes before you and will be with you; he will never leave you nor forsake you. Do not be afraid; do not be discouraged."

EXERCISE: You were suddenly hit by a bus . . .

Imagine that you were unable to lead for a significant period of time. OK, you were just hit by a bus! Who are the people around you who you would most likely delegate ministry assignments? Identify the person and write their assignment.

PERSON   ASSIGNMENTS

_____:_____

_____:_____

_____:_____

_____:_____

_____:_____

_____:_____

_____:_____

_____:_____

_____:_____

_____:_____

_____:_____

EXPOSURE: Identifying your successor

Now long before Moses announced Joshua as his successor to lead the Israelites into the Promise Land, Moses had to identify his successor. God clearly had Joshua appointed as Moses' successor, but how did

Moses come to identify his successor? How do you identify others in the congregation who can lead?

Dale Carnegie, American writer and lecturer, was a master at identifying potential leaders. Once asked by a reporter how he managed to hire forty-three-millionaires, Carnegie responded that the men had not been millionaires when they started working for him. They had become millionaires as a result. The reporter next wanted to know how he had developed these men to become such valuable leaders. Carnegie replied, *"Men are developed the same way gold is mined. Several tons of dirt must be moved to get an ounce of gold. But you don't go to the mine looking for dirt,"* he added. *"You go looking for the gold."* This is exactly the way you look for potential leaders.

Finding potential leaders is like finding gold. You've got to look beyond the dirt to see the valuable resource within a person. Here are five things you ought to look for in someone you have hopes of developing as a leader. To find your *"Joshua,"* look for someone who exhibits F. A. I. T. H.

Faithful. Look for someone who is faithful in following through on what they say they will do. You are looking for someone who is faithful in doing the little things.

Jesus gives us the Little then Much principle in Matthew 25:23. *"You have been faithful with a few things; I will put you in charge of many things."*

Available. Look for someone who makes themselves available. They show up. They show up on time. They make themselves available to learning new things.

Intentional. In other words, they are purposeful. They are focused and show follow-through. They don't quit easily.

Teachable. Look for someone who doesn't think he knows it all. Look for someone who is eager to learn more than she knows already. Is the person open to receiving feedback?

Humble. Is the person willing to serve, and serve behind the scenes? I always have reservations about people who only want to serve in the spotlight.

EXERCISE: Identify potential leaders

Identify two potential leaders by looking for F.A.I.T.H.

Name of person #1: _____

How does this person demonstrate faithfulness?

_____

_____

How does this person demonstrate availability?

_____

_____

How do you see this person as being intentional?

_____

_____

How does this person demonstrate a teachable spirit?

_____

_____

How does this person demonstrate humility?

_____

_____

Name of person #2: _____

How does this person demonstrate faithfulness?

_____

_____

How does this person demonstrate availability?

_____

_____

How do you see this person as being intentional?

_____

_____

How does this person demonstrate a teachable spirit?

_____

_____

How does this person demonstrate humility?

_____

_____

EXPOSURE: Developing your successor

Once you identify a potential leader, or your successor, you need to develop this future leader. Moses modeled leadership for Joshua. Moses mentored Joshua by providing instruction to Joshua. Eventually Moses motivated Joshua to lead himself by giving Joshua assignments so that he could sharpen his skills as a developing leader.

In this Exposure section we're going to look at a process for developing leaders made popular by John Maxwell in his book, *Developing the*

Leaders Around You. Here are five steps for developing the people around you and your successor. Here's how you can develop your own Joshua.

1. MODEL: *"I do, you watch, we talk."*

Do you remember when you were in school, especially in the younger grades, when your teacher invited you to bring something into the classroom and tell the other students about it? What was that called? It was called "Show & Tell," wasn't it? "Show & Tell" is a very effective teaching technique.

So often we want to tell people how to do something, when one of the most effective ways to help someone learn is to show them, and then tell them. That's why the first step in developing people is to model for them what we want them to be able to do.

This is what Moses did for Joshua. *"Moses set out with Joshua his aide, and Moses went up on the mountain of God."* (Exodus 24:13) Moses often invited Joshua to be with him to learn from him by observing how Moses led.

This is, in fact, how Jesus developed people, how Jesus discipled people. He invited people to "come and follow," to be with Him. Jesus modeled for them what He wanted them to know and what He wanted them to do. For instance, in John 13, Jesus modeled for his disciples what it means to be a servant by getting down on his knees and washing his disciples' feet like a common house servant. Jesus then said to them, *"I have set you an example that you should do as I have done for you."* (John 13:15)

When you are developing someone, discipling someone, start with the modeling step. *"I do, you watch, we talk."* After you've modeled, find a time when you can ask:

- *What did you observe?*
- *Did you learn anything by watching?*
- *Can you imagine you being able to do this in the future?*

2. MENTOR: *"I do, you help, we talk."*

After Joshua had spent some time with Moses, Joshua became Moses' helper. Numbers 11:28 says, *"Joshua, son of Nun, who had been Moses' aide since youth, spoke up and said, 'Moses, my lord, stop them!'"* Joshua began serving as Moses' helper or aide.

In the mentoring step, you ask the person to help you. You give them a small assignment to see how they do. You stay close by to help them if they run into any difficulty or need any help. One of the ways I mentor potential small group leaders is to have them share a brief testimony during the group time, or I will have them co-teach a small portion of the lesson with me.

After the assignment, you sit down with the person to see how the assignment went. Here are four mentoring questions to ask:

- *How did you think it went?*
- *What do you think worked?*
- *What didn't work?*
- *How do you think we could improve?*

3. MOTIVATE: *"You do, I help, we talk."*

At this step, we exchange places. You invite the person to take the lead while you help. Typically, the person will say something like, *"I'm not sure I can do it by myself."* At this step what the person needs more than anything else is encouragement. So be positive and very encouraging as young developing leaders need it. Remind the developing leader that you're close by to help if they find themselves in trouble.

In Deuteronomy 1:38, God says to Moses, *"Your assistant, Joshua son of Nun, will enter it. Encourage him, because he will lead Israel to inherit it."* The word *"encouragement"* is made up of two words: *"en"* and *"courage."* To encourage is to put your courage, your strong positive belief about the person, into that person.

To effectively encourage, you've got to believe in people before they believe in themselves! To effectively encourage, you've got to believe in people before they are successful! Anyone can believe in someone after they've been successful. A real encourager encourages people before they are successful.

Moses, not only encouraged Joshua privately, he encouraged Joshua publicly. It is important for the leader to encourage and endorse a developing leader publicly. It is important for the developing leader and the congregation to hear you say to the developing leader, *"I believe in you!"* When you come to the place where you have confidence in the developing leader to lead, you are ready to move to the next step.

4. MONITOR: *"You do, I watch, we talk."*

At the monitor step you are saying, *"You can do this without me. You don't need my help. I'll just watch, and we can talk about it after. But you are ready to do this by yourself."*

Moses did this for Joshua when he gave Joshua the assignment of spying out the Promise Land. Twelve spies went into the land of Canaan, with ten returning with a negative report and only Joshua and Caleb returning with a *"we can do it"* positive report.

One of the things that Moses observed about Joshua was faith and confidence in God. In Numbers 14:6-9 we read: *"Joshua son of Nun and Caleb son of Jephunneh, who were among those who had explored the land, tore their clothes and said to the entire Israelite assembly, 'The land we passed through and explored is exceedingly good. If the LORD is pleased with us, he will lead us into that land, a land flowing with milk and honey, and will give it to us. Only do not rebel against the LORD. And do not be afraid of the people of the land, because we will swallow them up. Their protection is gone, but the LORD is with us. Do not be afraid of them.'"*

Joshua had incredible faith in God. Numbers 32:12 says that Joshua followed the Lord *"wholeheartedly."* Not *"half-heartedly"* but *"wholeheartedly."* Joshua proved himself to be a strong leader who followed God *"wholeheartedly."*

After the assignment, honest feedback is crucial for the developing leader. If you hope to develop as a leader, seek feedback from others. We might be hesitant to seek feedback for fear that the critique might feel too painful. But if you want to grow as a leader, and continue to develop as a leader, you've got to seek honest feedback.

If you are providing feedback after someone has completed an assignment, give feedback carefully. Giving feedback is not as simple as telling someone all the things you felt they did wrong. Giving helping feedback requires sensitivity and a skill set that comes only with practice.

In providing feedback, first be sure to affirm several things that the person did well. Be as specific as possible as you affirm what the person did well. Only after you have affirmed that the person did several things well, you could say, *"If there was one thing that could significantly improve your ministry, it would be . . . ."* Choose one thing that you want to focus on for improvement. Take the time to explain specifically what they could do to improve. Then finish with one or two more things you would affirm, so that the words about how improvement could come are sandwiched between the affirmations.

5. MULTIPLY: *"You do, someone else watches, you talk"*

In this final step, you are inviting the person you developed to do the same thing for someone else what you did for them, starting with modeling.

EXERCISE: Developing the people around you

Identify three people in your sphere of influence and the step that they are at in leadership development. Then identify what you might invite them to do to progress as a leader.

	Name	Step	Next Step Assignment
1.	_____	_____	_____
2.	_____	_____	_____
3.	_____	_____	_____

EXPOSURE: Giving up the reins is not easy

Moses' desire to cross over the Jordan with his people is evident in his own words found in Deuteronomy 3:23-25: *"23 At that time I pleaded with the Lord: 24 "Sovereign LORD, you have begun to show to your servant your greatness and your strong hand. For what god is there in heaven or on earth who can do the deeds and mighty works you do? 25 Let me go over and see the good land beyond the Jordan—that fine hill country and Lebanon."*

Moses may have been thinking that even if he wasn't allowed to lead the Israelites into the land, God did not say that he couldn't simply enter the land. God, however, made it quite clear that Moses' time leading had truly come to an end, and Moses had to make peace with the fact that Joshua was going to succeed him.

God responded directly to Moses and cut him off with the words, *"26 But because of you the LORD was angry with me and would not listen to me. "That is enough," the LORD said. "Do not speak to me anymore about this matter."* (Deuteronomy 3:27)

How difficult it is for leaders to acknowledge when their time has come. Most attempt to hang on to any vestige of power or position, and often this is simply futile. Letting go of the reins is one of the most difficult tests for every leader.

Top leaders are often known for their powerful egos, without which things wouldn't get done. But this ego can make leaders reluctant to let go of the reins, especially when their successors are inexperienced and somewhat reticent to assert themselves. But the wise, experienced leader is convinced that the organization's future—it's survival and success— are more important that personal success. Wise, experienced leaders know the importance of passing on the baton to the next generation of leaders. They know that without a successor, there is no long-term success.

Most leaders find it difficult to accept that their role has run its course and that they will not accomplish all their goals. It wasn't easy for Moses to accept the news that he would not be leading the people into the Promised Land. Most leaders are not satisfied with fulfilling only part of their dream. Perhaps this is why God commanded Moses to *"27 Go up to the top of Pisgah and look west and north and south and east. Look at the land with your own eyes, since you are not going to cross this Jordan."* (Deuteronomy 3:27)

Perhaps God hoped that Moses would recognize just how far he—and the people he had led—had come. Standing on the top of Pisgah, all Moses had to do is turn around and gaze at the desert behind them to realize the miraculous nature of their journey.

All leaders reach a point at which they can no longer serve their people in the same way as they have done earlier in their leadership journey. New leadership is needed. The individual who possessed the abilities to lead them from Egypt to the shore of the Jordan was not necessarily the one to be their leader once they settled in the land. A different set of skills and a different vision were needed.

But God had been preparing for this. Joshua was going to lead the Israelites into the Promise Land. So, God directed Moses to, *"28 commission Joshua, and encourage and strengthen him, for he will lead this people across and will cause them to inherit the land that you will see."* (Deuteronomy 3:28) To prepare Joshua to take his place, God commanded Moses to *"encourage and strengthen him"* as he would now be leading the people across the Jordan into the Promise Land.

God emphasized that Moses' role at this point was to encourage and strengthen Joshua in order to prepare his protégé for the tough task of leading. In doing so, Moses taught his people one of the most important lessons by leaving them. For the goal of the leader is to make himself or herself superfluous.

After serving forty-two years in pastoral ministry, the past thirty of those years serving the First Baptist Church of Everett, Washington, I shared with the leadership and congregation that I had felt God's leading to pass the baton on to their next pastor. I spent my last months teaching from the book of Exodus about the journey toward the Promise Land, and encouraged the members of the congregation to consider that their most exciting days would be in their future. As difficult as it was, I explained to the members of the church that upon my last day serving as their pastor, I would no longer be their pastor and would not preach, or perform weddings or funerals for the congregation. I wanted to give their future *Joshua* the space to lead, out from under my shadow.

Every leader will pass the leadership baton to the next leader. In the book NEXT, the author makes the credible point that *"every leader is an interim leader."* (William Vanderbloemen and Warren Bird, *Next*, p.9) The only question is, how well will we do it. It requires a leader of strong character, maturity and humility to pass the leadership baton to a new leader, but Moses did it well. In addition to teaching and encouraging Joshua, he set Joshua up to succeed. But there is something else that needs to be done. The people have to be prepared to accept the next leader.

EXPOSURE: People must be prepared for succession

For a successful handoff, the congregation must be prepared. In Deuteronomy 31:1-6, we read how Moses prepared the Israelites for the passing of the leadership baton. Moses was still casting vision for the Israelites, motivating them to not be afraid but to be strong and courageous, and to see God as the One leading them; only Moses will not be leading them. Listen to this seasoned leader's words.

> *"1Then Moses went out and spoke these words to all Israel: 2 "I am now a hundred and twenty years old and I am no longer able to lead you. The Lord has said to me, 'You shall not cross the Jordan.' 3 The Lord your God himself will cross over ahead of you. He will destroy these nations before you, and you will take possession of their land. Joshua also will cross over ahead of you, as the Lord said. 4 And the Lord will do to them what he did to Sihon and Og, the kings of the Amorites, whom he destroyed along with their land. 5 The Lord will deliver them to you, and you must do to them all that I have commanded you. 6 Be strong and courageous. Do not be afraid or terrified because of them, for the Lord your God goes with you; he will never leave you nor forsake you."*

Moses was aware of just how important his actions were at this crucial junction in the people's journey.

The people needed clarity and encouragement. He provided this by explaining to the people, that while he would not be going with them, they did not need to fear the Canaanites because God was their true Leader. Joshua was God's earthly representative, and God's favor had been demonstrated in their recent victory over Sihon and Og. You and I can hear his attempt to reassure their future as he spoke, *"3 The Lord your God himself will cross over ahead of you. He will destroy these nations before you, and you will take possession of their land."*

Moses understood that the people's needs overshadowed his own immediate personal needs, and this shows Moses to be a true leader—one primarily concerned and devoted to his flock.

Then Moses did something quite significant. Moses called to Joshua to stand beside him *"in the presence of all Israel."* We read about this in Deuteronomy 31:7-8.

> *"7 Then Moses summoned Joshua and said to him in the presence of all Israel, "Be strong and courageous, for you must go with this people into the land that the Lord swore to their ancestors to give them, and you must divide it among them as their inheritance. 8 The Lord himself goes before you and will be with you; he will never leave you nor forsake you. Do not be afraid; do not be discouraged."*

This public act of *"calling,"* in which Moses stated that it will be Joshua who would be leading the people into the land, is an important step in the passing of the baton, or the mantle of leadership. Moses gave his successor as much personal support as he could, including emphasizing that Joshua would play the role of not only leading them into the land, but also appropriating the land to each tribe.

God then commanded Moses to call Joshua once again, so that both of them could enter the Tabernacle. It was in the Tabernacle, in the presence of the entire community, and in the presence of God, that the transfer of leadership to Joshua took place. *"14 The LORD said to Moses, "Now the day of your death is near. Call Joshua and present yourselves at the tent of meeting, where I will commission him." So, Moses and Joshua came and presented themselves at the tent of meeting."* (Deuteronomy 31:14)

In addition to announcing Joshua as his successor, Moses did something else that helped the Israelites accept Joshua as their new leader. Moses commissioned Joshua to lead the people of Israel in a very public ceremony. We read about it in Numbers 27:22-23. *"Moses did as the LORD commanded him. He took Joshua and had him stand before Eleazar the priest and the whole assembly. Then he laid his hands on him and commissioned him, as the LORD instructed through Moses."* Moses publicly handed over the keys to Joshua.

In every congregation there are symbols of blessing and the confirming of authority to lead: commissioning, ordination, laying on of hands, or what I call *"platform time"* where the new leader is seen ministering with blessing and confirmation. These symbols are not insignificant. They mark the official transfer of the leadership baton to the new leader, the transfer of responsibility, authority and accountability.

Joshua was ready to lead when the time came because Moses had taken the time to pour his life into Joshua. Moses developed Joshua, and passed the leadership baton to Joshua, so that Deuteronomy 34:9 says, *"Now Joshua son of Nun was filled with the spirit of wisdom because Moses had laid his hands on him. So the Israelites listened to him and did what the LORD had commanded Moses."* I believe that much of Joshua's success as a leader was due to the effective leadership of his mentor, Moses.

But now, Joshua was the leader of the Israelites. Becoming a leader is not the final goal of the leader developing process. The goal should be to develop leaders who are committed and capable of developing other leaders. The real goal is to see leaders who multiply themselves.

Like all great leaders, Moses continued to mentor Joshua up until his death, sharing with him the lessons he had learned about leadership. On the day of his death, Moses' last act was to write down the whole Torah, which he had conveyed to the people and invited them to read every seven years in the presence of the entire people. Deuteronomy 31:9-11 tells us:

> *9 So Moses wrote down this law and gave it to the Levitical priests, who carried the ark of the covenant of the LORD, and to all the elders of Israel. 10 Then Moses commanded them: "At the end of every seven years, in the year for canceling debts, during the Festival of Tabernacles, 11 when all Israel comes to appear before the LORD your God at the place he will choose, you shall read this law before them in their hearing.*

A time will come in the process of developing a successor when it will be important for you to make a more public announcement of the developing leader's role. This is important for the developing leader as it will signify the mentoring leader's affirmation and blessing of the developing leader. It is important for the congregation to know so that this newer leader has the mentoring leader's blessing.

EXPOSURE: *Finishing well as a leader*

The Israelite's journey from Kadesh and Be'er led them to the shore of the Jordan River, just east of the Land of Canaan. Before they could cross the Jordan, they defeated the Amorites. In the final chapter of Deuteronomy, chapter 34, we read about Moses' last days. Moses was 120 years old at the time, when he climbed Nebo from the plains of Moab to the top of Pisgah.

The summit of Mount Pisgah reaches a height of 4,500 feet. From the top of Mount Pisgah, almost a mile high, God allowed him to see the Promise Land. Then shortly after, Moses, at age one hundred and twenty, died there in Moab and was buried.

Deuteronomy 34:8-9 read: *"8 The Israelites grieved for Moses in the plains of Moab thirty days, until the time of weeping and mourning was over. 9 Now Joshua son of Nun was filled with the spirit of wisdom because Moses had laid his hands on him. So the Israelites listened to him and did what the Lord had commanded Moses."* Moses lived his life of influence to the very end as a leader. And Moses' influence as a leader continues!

This book of Deuteronomy concludes with these words of tribute about Moses, the leader: *"Since then, no prophet has risen in Israel like Moses, whom the Lord knew face to face, who did all those miraculous signs and wonders the Lord sent him to do in Egypt—to Pharaoh and to all his officials and to his whole land. For no one has ever shown the mighty power*

or performed the awesome deeds that Moses did in the sight of all Israel."
(Deuteronomy 34:10-12)

Moses finished well! Moses completed the work that God had given him
to do, and then he died. It was said of David, who later served as King
of Israel, *"When David had served God's purpose in his own generation, he
fell asleep."* (Acts 13:36) What greater tribute could be given to a leader
than the words, *"He completed the work that God had for him to do!"* Or
"She served God's purpose in the time that God gave her!"

So, to all of you, my partners in ministry, I want to leave you with these
final words of challenge:

> *"Lead well! Lead diligently! Lead well and diligently to the end!"*

No leader is perfect. Moses was far from perfect. Every leader makes
mistakes. Moses certainly made plenty of mistakes. But God's standard
for a leader has never been perfection. God has always chosen ordinary
people to accomplish His extraordinary work. To those God gives
the gift and/or the role of leadership, God's charge to you is found in
Romans 12:8. If God's gift or role for you *"is to lead, do it diligently."*
(TNIV)

Leading well and diligently to the end should be the aspiration of every
God-appointed leader. But the development of such a leader is a process,
a life-long process. Great leaders are committed to being learners for
life. They see every experience of leading as a learning experience.
They embrace the lessons, even painful lessons, in the hope of growing
to be a more effective leader like Jesus. As you continue to lead in the
endeavors to which God has called you, keep yourself open to God's
leader-shaping opportunities and lead courageously and diligently! God
bless you!

EXERCISE: *How do you imagine you will finish?*

Write your own five to ten sentence obituary, putting into it what you imagine will be your lifelong accomplishments and what you would want people to most remember about you as a leader. Share your obituary with a small group of three to four people.

_____

_____

_____

_____

_____

_____

_____

_____

_____

_____

_____

_____

_____

_____

_____

_____

_____

_____

_____

_____

_____

_____

BIBLIOGRAPHY

Anderson, Leith. Leadership That Works. Minneapolis: Bethany House Publishers, 1999.

Barna, George. Turning Vision Into Action. Ventura: Regal Books, 1996.

Barna, George. Leaders on Leadership. Ventura: Regal Books, 1997.

Barna, George. The Power of Vision. Ventura: Regal Books, 1992.

Beausay, William. The Leadership Genius of Jesus. Nashville: Thomas Nelson Publishing, 1997. Belasco, James A./Stayer, Ralph C., Flight of the Buffalo. New York: Warner Books, 1993 Bennis, Warren/ Nanus, Burt. Leaders: Strategies For Taking Charge. New York: Harper and Row Publishers, 1997.

Black, J. Stewart/Gregersen, Hal. Leading Strategic Change. Upper Saddle River: Prentice Hall, 2003.

Blackaby, Henry. Experiencing God. Nashville: B & H Publishing Group, 2008.

Bridges, William. Managing Transitions: Making the Most of Change. Cambridge: Perseus Books, 1991

Clinton, J. Robert. Making of a Leader. Colorado Springs: NavPress, 1988.

Cloud, Henry. Changes That Heal. Grand Rapids: Zondervan. 1992.

Cohen, Norman J. Moses and the Journey to Leadership. Woodstock, VT: Jewish Lights Publishing, 2007

Cordeiro, Wayne. Doing Church As A Team. Ventura: Regal, 2001.

DePree, Max. Leadership is an Art. Broadway: Dell Publishing Group, Inc., 1989.

Ford, Leighton. Transforming Leadership. Downers Grove: InterVarsity Press, 1991.

Forman, Rowland/Jones, Jeff/Miller, Bruce. The Leadership Baton. Grand Rapids: Zondervan, 2004.

Fromm, Erich. The Fear of Freedom. London: Routledge & Kegan Paul, 1942.

Gladwell, Malcolm. The Tipping Point. Little, Brown and Company, 2000.

Goleman, Daniel/Boyatzis, Richard/McKee, Annie. Primal Leadership. Boston: Harvard Business School Press, 2002.

Greenlead, Robert K. The Servant as Leader. Mahwah Paulist, 1977.

Herrington, Jim/Bonem, Mike/Furr, James. Leading Congregational Change. San Francisco: Jossey-Bass. 2000.

Hybels, Bill. Axiom: Powerful Leadership Proverbs. Grand Rapids: Zondervan, 2008.

Hybels, Bill. Courageous Leadership. Grand Rapids: Zondervan, 2002.

Kotter, J. P. Leading Change. Boston: Harvard Business School Press, 1996.

Kotter, John/Rathgeber, Holger. Our Iceberg is Melting. New York: St. Martin's Press, 2005. Kouzes, James/Posner, Barry. Credibility. San Francisco: Jossey-Bass, 2003.

Kouzes, James/Posner, Barry. The Truth About Leadership. San Francisco: Jossey-Bass, 2010. Logan, Dave/King, John/Fischer-Wright, Halee. Tribal Leadership. New York: Harper Collins Publishers, 2008.

MacMillan, Pat. The Performance Factor. Nashville: Broadman & Holman Publishers, 2001. Mancini, Will. Church Unique. San Francisco: Jossey-Bass, 2008.

Maxwell, John. Developing the Leaders Around You. Nashville: Thomas Nelson, Inc., 1995.

Maxwell, John. Winning With People. Nashville: Thomas Nelson Publishing, 2004.

Maxwell, John. Thinking for a Change. Warner Books, 2003.

Maxwell, John. The 21 Irrefutable laws of Leadership. Nashville: Thomas Nelson, Inc., 1998. Maxwell, John. The 17 Indisputable Laws of Teamwork. Nashville: Thomas Nelson, Inc., 2001. Maxwell, John. Failing Forward. Nashville: Thomas Nelson, Inc., 2000.

Maxwell, John/Dornan, Jim. Becoming a Person of Influence. Nashville: Thomas Nelson, Inc., 1997.

Maxwell, John. Talent is Never Enough. Nashville: Thomas Nelson, Inc., 2007.

Nelson, Allan/Appel, Gene. How to Change Your Church. Nashville: Word Publishing, 2000. Ortberg, John. If You Want to Walk on Water, You've Got to Get Out of the Boat. Grand Rapids: Zondervan Publishing House, 2001.

Putman, Jim. Church Is a Team Sport. Grand Rapids: Baker Books, 2008.

Rainer, Thom/Geiger, Eric. Simple Church. Nashville: B & H Publishing Group, 2006.

Rainey, Dennis/Rainey, Barbara. Building Your Mate's Self-Esteem. Nashville: Thomas Nelson, Inc., 1995.

Sanders, J. Oswald. Spiritual Leadership. Chicago: Moody Press, 1980.

Schaller, Lyle. The Change Agent. Nashville: Abingdon, 1972.

Stanley, Andy. The Next Generation Leader. Sisters: Multnomah Publishers, 2003.

Stanley, Andy. Visioneering. Sisters: Multnomah Publishers, 1999.

Swindoll, Charles. Hand Me Another Brick. Nashville: Thomas Nelson Publishers, 1978.

Swindoll, Charles. Moses. Nashville: Word Publishing, 1999.

Vanderbloemen, Willian/Bird, Warren. Next. Grand Rapids, MI: Baker Books, 2014.

Warren, Rick. The Purpose Driven Church. Grand Rapids: Zondervan, 1995.